Dickey, Jeff, author.
Write modern web
apps with the MEAN
stack

Write Modern Web Apps
with the MEAN Stack

Mongo, Express, AngularJS, and Node.js

D0702171

DEVELOP AND DESIGN

Jeff Dickey

 PEACHPIT PRESS
WWW.PEACHPIT.COM

Write Modern Web Apps with the MEAN Stack: Mongo, Express, AngularJS, and Node.js
Jeff Dickey

Peachpit Press

www.peachpit.com

To report errors, please send a note to errata@peachpit.com
Peachpit Press is a division of Pearson Education.

Copyright © 2015 by Jeff Dickey

Editor: Kim Wimpsett
Production editor: David Van Ness
Proofreader: Liz Welch
Technical editor: Joe Chellman
Compositor: Danielle Foster
Indexer: Danielle Foster
Cover design: Aren Straiger
Interior design: Mimi Heft

Notice of Rights

All rights reserved. No part of this book may be reproduced or transmitted in any form by any means, electronic, mechanical, photocopying, recording, or otherwise, without the prior written permission of the publisher. For information on getting permission for reprints and excerpts, contact permissions@peachpit.com.

Notice of Liability

The information in this book is distributed on an "As Is" basis, without warranty. While every precaution has been taken in the preparation of the book, neither the author nor Peachpit shall have any liability to any person or entity with respect to any loss or damage caused or alleged to be caused directly or indirectly by the instructions contained in this book or by the computer software and hardware products described in it.

Trademarks

Many of the designations used by manufacturers and sellers to distinguish their products are claimed as trademarks. Where those designations appear in this book, and Peachpit was aware of a trademark claim, the designations appear as requested by the owner of the trademark. All other product names and services identified throughout this book are used in editorial fashion only and for the benefit of such companies with no intention of infringement of the trademark. No such use, or the use of any trade name, is intended to convey endorsement or other affiliation with this book.

ISBN-13: 978-0-13-393015-3
ISBN-10: 0-13-393015-7

9 8 7 6 5 4 3 2 1

Printed and bound in the United States of America

To Mom and Dad,
for sometimes allowing me to sit inside all day on that computer

ABOUT THE AUTHOR

Jeff Dickey is a full-stack web developer with years of startup experience in San Francisco and Los Angeles. Jeff has launched projects, maintained large systems, and led development teams. With more than 10 years of experience on all of the major web platforms, he is continually searching for the latest technology for building applications. Currently Jeff works for Heroku as its first CLI developer. Jeff is also an instructor for General Assembly, teaching a course on back-end web development.

CONTENTS

PREFACE

WHO IS THIS BOOK FOR?

This book is for web developers wanting to learn how building web applications has changed. The book assumes a basic knowledge of JavaScript. Knowledge of Node or Angular is helpful as well but not required.

WHY I WROTE THIS BOOK

I've been a web developer since 2004 and have professionally worked with most of the major web platforms. I love to seek out new technology that helps me write my applications better.

Applications built with an MVC framework such as Angular has been the largest paradigm shift that I've seen in the web community. Frameworks and tools have come and gone, but client-side MVC applications are fundamentally different.

I've been impressed with the quality of applications that I've shipped with Angular and Node. The tools are simple—sometimes a bit naïve—but this simplicity comes with the fantastic ability to iterate on features and maintain a codebase.

Applications such as those built with the MEAN stack are becoming more popular, but many development teams still feel comfortable with server-generated pages and relational databases.

I've had such good luck with MEAN applications that I want to share my knowledge of how to build them with you.

I hope you'll enjoy exploring this new method of building applications with me. I love discussing these topics, so feel free to reach out to me on Twitter to continue the conversation.

Jeff Dickey
@dickeyxxx
August 2014

INTRODUCTION

The JavaScript community has a strong belief in the power of composability when architecting software. This is in line with the Unix philosophy of simple components that can be used together to quickly build applications.

By no means is this methodology the only one that exists. Ruby on Rails, for example, uses an opinionated framework to make decisions for you about what your application should look like. Opinionated frameworks offer the advantage of being able to quickly learn an application because out of the box it works—you just need to fill in the gaps. Opinionated frameworks are also easier to learn because there is usually a "right" way to do something. The downside is that you're limited to building applications that the framework was made for, and moving outside of the use cases the framework was made for can be difficult.

By contrast, the composition methodology is more flexible. Composing simple pieces together has a clear advantage of allowing you to build anything you want. These frameworks provide you with building blocks, and it's up to you to decide how to put them together. The downside is mostly in the learning phase. It's difficult to know what is a good idea and what is a bad idea without having experience doing both.

For this reason, it's useful to read up on opinionated guides for how to build JavaScript applications. These opinions provide one person's viewpoint on good and bad decisions and give you a road map to what an application should look like.

This book shows you how to build your own MEAN application following my opinions of what a good application should look like. These opinions come from my experience developing applications. While I have a good amount of experience, it's unlikely it will fit perfectly with any other one person. For this reason, I find books such as this are useful to learn not just the "how" of using a tool set but the "why" as well.

In other words, it's useful to know how to use promises in Node but not very useful if you don't understand why they're useful.

The application you will build is called simply Social App (see **Figure I.1**). You can see an example of it running at *https://mean-sample.herokuapp.com* as well as the code at *https://github.com/dickeyxxx/mean-sample*.

The application is similar to Twitter. Users can create an account and add posts. The feature count is not large but does consist of some neat solutions such as WebSockets that immediately display new posts to all users viewing the application. I'll also go over compiling the CSS and JavaScript assets with Gulp, deploying the application to both Heroku and Digital Ocean, building a clean, maintainable API and more.

Having a "newsfeed" that displays live, updating content is a pattern that I see on just about every project I work on. I chose this as an example because it is complicated enough to incorporate many different tools but not so complex that you will become bogged down in the minutiae of this specific application.

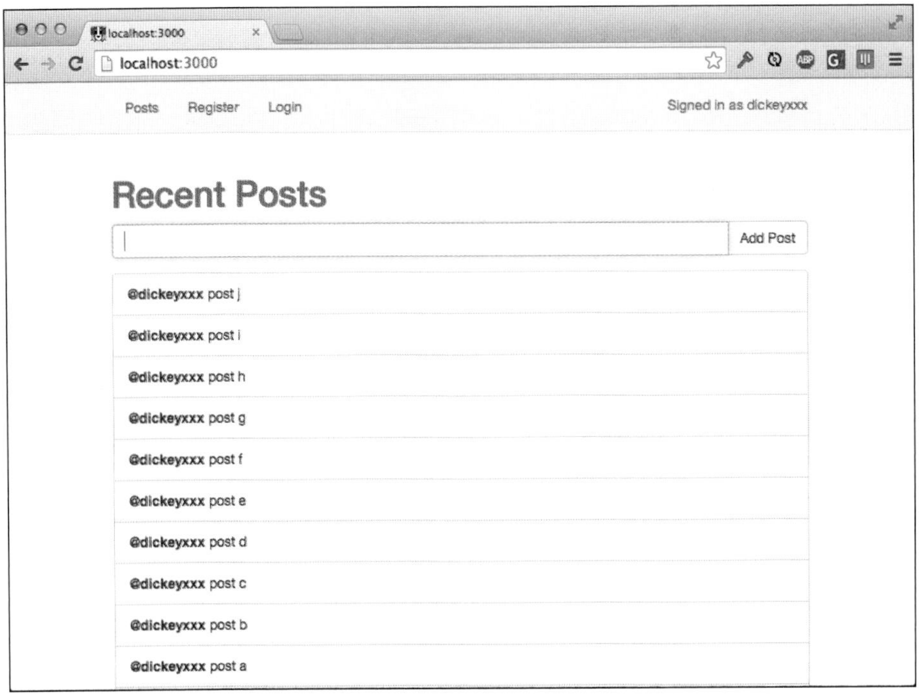

FIGURE I.1 Social app

This application is also easily extensible. I encourage you while reading this book to take the time to not only implement the application as I have done but to build features of your own. It's relatively easy to follow along and build the same application, but you know that's not how software is actually written.

Learning a new skill is tough. As a teacher, I've witnessed many people learning something for the first time and been able to witness their progress. One facet of that I've noticed is that learning doesn't feel like anything. You can't tell whether you're learning something when you're learning it—in fact, learning feels a lot more like frustration.

What I've learned is that during this period of frustration is actually when people improve the most, and their improvements are usually obvious to an outsider. If you feel frustrated while trying to understand these new concepts, try to remember that it might not feel like it, but you're probably rapidly expanding your knowledge.

With that, join me in Chapter 1 while you learn a bit about the history of the Web's surprising relationship with JavaScript, how it's changed the way we think of applications, and where the MEAN stack fits in.

How Modern Web Architecture Is Changing

In this chapter, I'll cover how web applications were developed in the past, examine how JavaScript has evolved, and talk about the new approach web developers are taking toward architecture.

THE RISE OF THE STATIC APP

Web applications for about the last 10 years have looked similar. They typically follow a three-tier architecture consisting of a database, a server that generates HTML, and a browser that renders the HTML.

To deliver a dynamic application, traditional applications follow this process:

1. The user's browser sends a request to a web URL. To make this happen, the user either clicks an anchor <a> tag or types in a URL.
2. The server receives the request and then fetches data from a database to fulfill it.
3. The server uses the data to generate an HTML response and returns the response to the browser.

Whether you're talking about applications developed in Java, Ruby, Python, C#, or any other back-end language, this is how applications are served. Some applications may be more efficient when performing these tasks, but all applications perform all three steps.

AJAX-EMPOWERED JAVASCRIPT

JavaScript has been included in browsers for a while but really hasn't been taken seriously until the last few years. A big change for JavaScript was the development of Ajax (Asynchronous JavaScript and XML). Ajax allowed developers to perform web requests as mentioned earlier, but instead of doing a full-page reload, they could asynchronously grab XML from a server and then cause the page to react. Later, developers started formatting data using the much-simpler JSON (JavaScript Object Notation). Today, JSON is virtually the only format used. We still use the term Ajax to refer to this functionality because the object used for this task is called XMLHttpRequest, but it doesn't require XML.

Google's Gmail and Google Maps were two of the first applications to leverage Ajax, and they were groundbreaking. Before Google Maps, looking at a map website involved clicking arrow keys that would do a slow (several-second) page reload to show a new area; there was no panning whatsoever.

PROGRESSIVE ENHANCEMENT

During the same period of the early, interactive Web, there was a strong idea of "progressive enhancement" that encouraged developers to write applications such that they would work whether or not JavaScript was enabled. Some users would use browsers that had no (or little) JavaScript support, and others would disable JavaScript because of security concerns.

Typically this means developers would "decorate" elements on a page with JavaScript so that they could use Ajax. If the browser did not have JavaScript, the page would use href attributes to perform the same action with a full-page refresh.

This meant developers had to build all of their features twice, once for JavaScript users and once for those without JavaScript. They had to test all of their functionality for both methods as well, and this way of working even held back certain kinds of functionality—features that simply could not be built without JavaScript.

Developers would often mock applications that supported users with JavaScript only. sighjavascript.tumblr.com is one example that is worth a look. Its latest post was only in September 2013, but it looks like a relic of the distant past. Today, though, no popular browser allows you to disable JavaScript, and even the simplest sites out there still require it. In other words, as a developer, you can now depend on JavaScript being enabled. Progressive enhancement held developers back quite a bit when crafting applications, but that is no longer a worry.

SPAGHETTI JAVASCRIPT

Another problem arose in the time when JavaScript wasn't taken seriously: maintenance. Applications began to explode with the size of JavaScript, and quickly there were a bunch of ad hoc JavaScript pieces littered through codebases. Standards for writing JavaScript well were practiced by only the most expert of JavaScript developers.

JavaScript was looked down upon, the sort of code you would write as little of as possible. When you had to fix something with JavaScript that another developer wrote, it typically meant tossing the code out the window and rewriting the feature completely.

Application codebases were bad, and developers needed structure to define their applications. They had learned this with server-side languages, so typically applications would have good structure and code on the server side (complete with automated tests) but would be extremely lacking on the front end. In fact, JavaScript testing frameworks have been around only since 2009.

MOBILE APIS

Along with Ajax, another change appeared in the development world: mobile. Native mobile applications quickly took over the development community and became arguably even more popular than their web counterparts.

Since mobile applications still often needed a back end, they would have to communicate with a server using some kind of an API to move data back and forth. Servers were already serving HTML, so this became a natural fit. Typically native mobile apps would send/receive JSON, while web browsers would send/receive HTML.

Developers would typically find themselves writing two interfaces to the same application, one for native mobile apps that worked via a REST-like API and another for the web browsers they already knew.

ENTER THE THICK CLIENT

Knowing that you can now generally depend on JavaScript being enabled in browsers, a new way to develop applications has begun. You can build *thick* clients that will do the heavy lifting (rather than the server doing most of that work) and interact with a server via an API (much in the way of a mobile client).

HOW MODERN WEB ARCHITECTURE WORKS

This flow works as follows:

1. The user's browser requests a static HTML page.
2. The HTML page contains JavaScript that builds the base structure of the page.
3. The JavaScript then performs Ajax to load content (typically JSON) via an API.
4. JavaScript then takes this content and modifies the DOM to represent the content.

The main difference with this method is that the angle brackets (HTML) are generated on the client, not on the server. This is a huge difference from the way applications were built in the past.

THE BENEFITS OF MODERN WEB ARCHITECTURE

This modern workflow has the following advantages:

- **Simpler back end**: As applications require only a single API to transmit/receive content, the same API used for mobile apps can now be used for the browser as well. It also turns out to be much easier to build software that speaks JSON than software that speaks HTML.
- **Performance**: Most of the work that servers do is building HTML pages. Moving that work to the client saves a tremendous amount of effort. The front-end code can be easily served by a CDN (content delivery network) that can quickly deliver the bootstrapping content anywhere in the world. Since the client no longer has to download and render complete pages, the performance on the user's end can be much greater as well.
- **Standardized tools**: Static applications are built with heavy amounts of JavaScript, HTML, and CSS. These are the building blocks of the Web and understood by all web developers.
- **Rapid prototyping**: Because the only requirement to build an application is front-end JavaScript, it is easy to mock up a web application. All the server data can be stubbed (or simply not saved), and you can focus on the user's experience. Later you can fill in the functionality with an API.
- **Increased modularity**: Since you no longer have one giant codebase (known in the Rails world as the *monorail*), you can break your application into logical pieces, each well suited to perform its specific task.

In this book, you will explore ways to develop applications in this thick-client fashion. You will be using four tools: MongoDB, Express, Angular.js, and Node.js (popularly known as the *MEAN stack*). Using these tools, with JavaScript to bind them together, you can quickly build fast applications that scale.

## CHAPTER 2

Why JavaScript Is a Good Choice for Modern Apps

In this chapter, I'll talk about the four components of the MEAN stack (MongoDB, Express.js, Angular.js, and Node.js) and get you all set up to start the project in the next chapter.

WHAT IS ANGULAR.JS?

Angular.js is a framework for building applications inside the browser. It is targeted toward highly interactive applications. Out of the box, it comes with many components useful for building applications. It also provides the structure for highly modular, testable applications.

You integrate it into an application by adding a `<script>` tag to the HTML and writing custom code that works inside it.

Some of the tools it includes are two-way data binding, a router, DOM manipulation, animations, dependency injection, testing utilities, Ajax helpers, and more.

It has a bit of a learning curve, but it allows you to build applications quickly that are easily maintainable.

HOW IS ANGULAR DIFFERENT THAN jQUERY?

Most web developers I know have a firm grasp of the JavaScript framework jQuery, so they often wonder what Angular does that jQuery cannot.

The fundamental difference between jQuery and Angular is imperative and declarative, respectfully. In jQuery, you apply JavaScript to manipulate the DOM, but in Angular you declare what the DOM should look like ahead of time.

jQuery was built for the progressive-enhancement Web. It is designed to augment an existing HTML page to provide interactivity. You start with a plain page and then apply selectors to make it dynamic.

In Angular, you build the page with Angular from the beginning. Instead of thinking "I have this element and I want to make it do X," you declare the page's structure based on the model.

As an example, if you had a `<ul>` like the following:

```
<ul>
 <li>Item 1</li>
 <li>Item 2</li>
 <li>Item 3</li>
</ul>
<button id='foo'>Add Item</button>
```

and you wanted to click the button to append an `<li>` to the list, you might implement that in jQuery like the following:

```
$('#foo').click(function() {
 $('ul').append('<li>Item 4</li>');
});
```

FIGURE 2.1 Example of this simple jQuery and Angular code

This works, but now the JavaScript has to know how to generate the <li>s just like the server that generated the HTML initially. This includes the entire markup such as special classes, inline styles, or other elements. Adding functionality such as real-time updating, deleting items, and styling items becomes difficult since all the code that adds, removes, and updates the <li>s has to stay in sync.

In Angular, instead you would let Angular build the <ul> using *directives*. The directives are special, custom HTML attributes that Angular understands that will change the HTML for you. These custom directives are one of the reasons people have called Angular *HTML6*.

The directive that would help you here is ng-repeat. It looks like the following:

```
<ul ng-controller='ListCtrl'>
 <li ng-repeat='item in list_items'>{{item}}</li>
</ul>
<button ng-click='addListItem()'>Add Item</button>
```

In the controller, you define an array called list_items, and the DOM will automatically update, showing an <li> for every item in the array. Note the ng-click directive as well. This allows the view to pass a click event to the controller. The controller would look like the following:

```
angular.module('app').controller('ListCtrl', function($scope) {
 $scope.list_items = [
    'Item 1',
    'Item 2',
    'Item 3'
 ];
 $scope.addListItem = function() {
   $scope.list_items.push('Item 4');
 };
});
```

Figure 2.1 shows this simple jQuery and Angular code in a browser.

In Angular, this is how you split the logic from the presentation (in jQuery, because you have to use DOM selectors, they are tied together). The controller simply manages one array by declaring it and declares a function that can append a new item to the array. The HTML defines how that array is represented in the DOM and what event triggers the add item function.

Note that nowhere in the code do you actually add an element to the list; this is the heart of the declarative style of Angular. You may notice the Angular example is more code, but that is the case only for simple examples. As soon as the logic becomes complex, Angular tends to be much more concise.

It turns out that in developing an application with the MEAN stack, much of your time is spent in Angular. There are a few reasons for this:

- You actually can depend on the browser to perform tasks. It's generally easier to perform logic directly rather than communicating it across web requests.
- JSON is spoken throughout. MongoDB, Node, and Angular all are written in, or "speak," JavaScript. JSON is essentially JavaScript and is great at speaking it as well. Also, in the SQL world you would have to perform heavy transformations to change the web request into SQL queries. Here, in the NoSQL world, the transformations are much simpler. Interactivity is easier. You'll simply be able to leverage the browser more than you could in a server-generated application. You'll be able to spend more time fine-tuning interactive functionality as opposed to "just making it work."

WHAT IS NODE.JS?

Node.js is a JavaScript runtime designed to be run outside of the browser. It is a general-purpose utility that can be used for many things, including asset compilation, scripting, monitoring, and most notably web servers.

Surprisingly, JavaScript has turned out to be a fantastic language for server-side web development. This is interesting since all of our client-side code has already been in JavaScript, and it wasn't originally intended to support back-end development. It's efficient both for development time and for performance.

While Node.js can be used for many things, for the purposes of this book assume when I say Node.js I am referring to back-end web servers written in Node.js specifically.

STARTUP VS. ENTERPRISE

In the last decade, we've had two general environments to choose from when it came to back-end development. We've had the enterprise environment typically using languages/platforms such as Java and C#. We've also had the startup environment with many languages/frameworks, including Rails, Django, and PHP.

These differences stem from the goals of teams in these environments. The goal of a startup is to validate the product as soon as possible. Shipping with bugs is better than not shipping. Delivering a product quickly allows a startup to dynamically alter itself to fit a need. Shipping takes priority over performance and maintainability.

The open source environment works great for startups or prototyping products, but scaling up these products is challenging. Duck typing, noncompiled scripting languages, code-as-documentation, and heavy use of metaprogramming are all trademarks of these platforms. Twitter famously started on the Rails stack and ran into many performance problems (remember the fail whale?) and in response migrated its platform to Java/Scala. Backward compatibility is much worse in the open source world as well.

The enterprise environment, on the other hand, is less interested in reaching market quickly but much more interested in maintainability and stability (read: performance). Where a startup might have to get to market quickly to validate an idea, an enterprise needs to ensure its product will work and that a developer will be able to pick it up in several years and be able to maintain it without a problem.

This shines through in the code. Hallmarks of enterprise platforms include compiler-checked code, heavy use of industry-standard patterns, verbosity over cleverness, and heavy documentation.

Node.js is unique because it works well for *both* the startup and enterprise environments.

FIGURE 2.2 The rise and fall of languages over the years

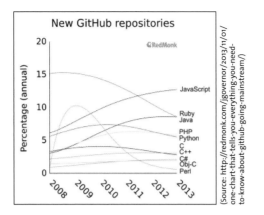

(Source: http://redmonk.com/jgovernor/2013/11/01/one-chart-that-tells-you-everything-you-need-to-know-about-github-going-mainstream/)

NODE.JS IN THE ENTERPRISE

At first glance, Node.js appears to be a startup-targeted platform because of its completely open source (not backed by a large corporation) scripting nature. Many companies have launched products quickly on the platform, making it well suited for product validation. That is remarkable success given the platform has been out for only five years.

Node.js is a great platform for startups, but it is even better for enterprise. I don't think Ryan Dahl had enterprise in mind when he built the platform, but it ended up being a perfect fit. Netflix, Groupon, SAP, LinkedIn, Microsoft, Yahoo!, Walmart, and PayPal are some of the enterprise companies that are using Node.js.

Yammer (part of Microsoft) was one of the first teams to tout it. The company labeled it scalable, fast to develop on, and having a vibrant ecosystem, according to *www.davetech. com/blog/notes-two-years-nodejs-yammer*.

PayPal has probably been Node's number-one fan in the enterprise. It's even hosting the first Node conference targeted specifically to enterprise (NodeDay). Bill Scott, PayPal's director of user experience, has commented many times on how Node has allowed PayPal to iterate much faster on products. PayPal is so fast in development now that he has teams work on four or five different products in tandem and implement only the best of the bunch. In the Java days, they would put all of their eggs in one basket and hope it worked out.

Most importantly, enterprise organizations have finally found a platform that developers like to work with. Developers are hard to find these days, so keeping the good ones around certainly involves keeping them happy. JavaScript has an enthusiastic community, which has quickly grown into the largest open source community by far. **Figure 2.2** shows a graph of how popular different languages have been over the years.

You can find a laundry list of companies using Node.js here: *https://github.com/joyent/node/wiki/Projects,-Applications,-and-Companies-Using-Node*.

FIGURE 2.3 Walmart
architect's Twitter feed

Eran Hammer @eranhammer · Nov 29

BREAKING NEWS: CPU on one server
touched 2% for 30 seconds. #nodebf

↩   ♺ 5   ★ 4   •••

Eran Hammer @eranhammer · Nov 29

I guess too nuts for anyone to guess: we
felt so good about everything, we
decided middle of Black Friday is perfect
time for a release.

↩   ♺ 12   ★ 12   •••

PERFORMANCE IN NODE.JS

Performance has been astounding on Node.js. Walmart reported that by moving to Node.
js it was able to double the number of requests per second and reduce response time by
35 percent, or 200ms. Walmart was so confident in its platform that it released it on Black
Friday, its busiest day of the year, to the entire mobile platform. Once it was online, Walmart
claimed the servers never went past 2 percent CPU utilization and had 200 million users
online (see **Figure 2.3**).

Walmart made the decision to move its entire platform to Node.js by the end of 2014. See
http://thechangelog.com/116/.

The reason Node.js is so fast is because of its architecture. Rather than going for a threading model popular in compiled languages or a process driven by one common in scripting
languages, Node.js chooses evented architecture.

EVENTED ARCHITECTURE

There are different ways to handle "concurrency" in software. The essential idea of concurrency is to allow multiple things to happen at the same time. This is common on servers
since more than one user will typically be accessing the server at the same time. Platforms
like Java will spawn a new thread on each connection. Threading is expensive, costing about
4MB of memory for each and limiting the number of threads that can be running at once. On
a 4GB server, this would be about 4,000 concurrent connections. It's also difficult to develop
platforms that are thread-safe allowing for that functionality.

Because of that complexity, languages such as Ruby, Python, and PHP do not have
threads (at least not threads that allow for real concurrency and without running custom
binaries). JavaScript also has a single-thread, but it is able to run multiple code paths in
parallel because of *events*.

Ryan Dahl, Node.js's creator, wanted a platform that was able to handle heavy amounts of I/O to build applications similar to Gmail where HTTP requests might have to sit around for long periods of time. Scripting languages are completely incapable of this, blocking the entire process when a web request arrives. Threaded systems can handle this to a point, but threads are still expensive.

JavaScript was designed to work within the confines of the browser. The most restrictive part of that was having a single thread and single process for the whole page. This meant that synchronous blocking in code would lock up a web page from all actions. JavaScript was built in this in mind. It is expressive when it comes to asynchronous code.

This style of handling I/O has worked well in the browser and is why Dahl chose it for building Node.js. As such, it can handle millions of concurrent requests on a single process.

Libraries that handle concurrency using events had been written in many other languages, such as Python's Twisted, Ruby's EventMachine, Akka for Java, and others. The difference here is JavaScript's syntax already assumes events through callbacks.

Running an entire application through a single thread is not a silver bullet, however. If you end up performing CPU-intensive (as opposed to I/O-intensive) work, the thread will be tied up, and everything will be blocked waiting for it to finish. Also, developers need to ensure that they do not allow errors to bubble up to the process, which would abort all current connections.

HOW CALLBACKS WORK

If you're new to this concept, basically the difference is that in most languages you'll ask the computer to do some I/O (database call, HTTP call, and so on) and then wait until it returns to continue your code path. Something like the following:

```
user = User.findById(100)
// Do something with user
```

This code will query the database for ID 100. It will pause that thread/process until the database comes back (which is relatively slow).

In JavaScript, this kind of code is rarely implemented. Typically what you'll do is pass an I/O call a "callback" that will need to be run when the task is completed. It would look like the following:

```
User.findById(100, function(user) {
  // Do something with user
});
```

The difference might seem subtle, but the important thing here is that while the database is fetching the result, that thread is free to do whatever else might be useful (take on another web request, listen to a different event, and so on).

A language like Ruby or Python would be stopped at this point. This is why you hear such good benchmarks about how scalable Node.js platforms are.

It's important to note that this doesn't make Node.js great for all use cases, just those with heavy I/O. It turns out that on the Web, that's usually what we're doing (transmitting via HTTP or waiting on a database).

MODULES AND NPM

In addition to callbacks, the other part of Node.js that everyone loves is the modules and packages available on NPM. The modules that Node.js has are really simple. Node.js uses a specification known as CommonJS.

CommonJS was developed as a way to declare external modules in JavaScript applications on the server. The general idea is that every file gets a `module.exports` object it can use to expose an object to others. If you had a file `foo.js`, you could expose a function like so:

```
var myFunc = function(input) {
    return input + ' world';
};
module.exports.foo = myFunc;
```

Then in a file `bar.js`, you could import that module like so:

```
var imported = require('./foo');
console.log(imported.foo('hello'));
// prints 'hello world'
```

On the Web, sharing code in JavaScript has always been a pain. Global variables are a common way to share code and are susceptible to conflict problems. This CommonJS spec is amazing because of its simplicity. Since dependencies are declared at runtime via the path, it's easy to diagnose dependency problems. This avoids dependency hell.

Having said that, I know when I first started using Node.js I didn't really "get it." It was simpler than I made it out to be. If you feel the same, don't worry; write a few code samples and modules down the road and you'll be feeling right at home.

Node.js's other best friend is NPM, which is the official package manager for Node.js and is now included in all Node.js installs.

If you've used Python's pip, Ruby's Bundler, or Java's Maven, it's similar to them. The nice thing about Node.js is that since it's so new, it was able to take the best bits of all of them.

Installing a package is easy. If you wanted to install, say, the mkdirp package that lets you create directories, you'd simply run the following:

```
npm install mkdirp
```

Then you can use mkdirp like so:

```
var mkdirp = require('mkdirp');

mkdirp('/tmp/foo/bar/baz', function (err) {
    if (err) console.error(err)
    else console.log('pow!')
});
```

I encourage you to read the "Introduction to NPM" at *http://howtonode.org/introduction-to-npm* to understand why NPM is made the way it is for a better understanding of its philosophy.

INSTALLING NODE.JS

Installing Node.js typically involves two parts: installing a base copy of Node.js and then installing a version switcher to choose the version of Node.js you want to use.

The reason for the switcher is that Node.js changes frequently. It's likely the version you get initially will not be the latest version. Also, once you get a couple of projects under your belt, you might have different projects that need different versions.

Follow these steps to get set up with Node.js for the project in this book:

1. To install the base version, use your package manager of choice.
   - For OS X with Homebrew (*http://brew.sh*), run brew install npm.
   - For Windows, visit *http://nodejs.org/download*.
   - For Ubuntu 13+, run sudo apt-get install npm.
   - For others, visit *https://github.com/joyent/node/wiki/Installing-Node.js-via-package-manager*.

2. Once you have the base version of Node.js installed, install the version switcher n by typing npm install -g n. The -g here denotes that you are installing the package globally. Otherwise, it would just install it into this directory and you couldn't just run y from anywhere.

To install and use the latest stable version of Node.js, use n stable. For more details on how to use n, see *https://www.npmjs.org/package/n*.

Now that you have Node.js installed, let's build a web server with it.

CREATING A VANILLA HTTP SERVER

Node.js has an HTTP module built in that can act as a server. A simple "Hello World" server would look like this in straight Node:

```
var http = require("http");
http.createServer(function(request, response) {
  response.writeHead(200, {"Content-Type": "text/plain"});
  response.write("Hello World");
  response.end();
}).listen(3000);
```

You'll need a server for the project in this book, so follow these steps:

1. Create the previous file anywhere and call it app.js.

   This responds to any route the web server receives. If you wanted to respond to others, you'd have to implement some kind of conditional on the request object.

2. Run the server by executing node app.js in a terminal. You won't see any output, but going to *http://localhost:3000* in your browser should display "Hello World."

   While exploring the code, pay attention to the createServer function. This is calling the function createServer on the HTTP module, passing in a new, anonymous function.

   The code inside that function is not executed right away but when the web server receives a new request. This is one of those callbacks discussed earlier in action. Node doesn't block at any part of this code; it just stores the function for use later when a request comes in.

   You could totally build an application like this, but the NPM package Express provides some nicer structure to common HTTP code. It's a lightweight web server (akin to Sinatra in Ruby, but even more low level).

WHAT IS EXPRESS?

Express is an NPM package for building web servers. It's by far the most common package used for building web applications with Node.js.

In Express, the same code for the web server would look like the following:

```
var express = require('express');
var app = express();

app.get('/', function(req, res) {
  res.send(200, 'Hello World');
});

app.listen(8888);
```

INSTALLING EXPRESS

Follow these steps to install Express:

1. Go ahead and put the previous code into a file called app-express.js.
2. Install Express into the directory by running npm install express.
3. Run the code simply by executing node app-express.js. You should then be able to access it at *http://localhost:8888* just like before.

As you can see, Express doesn't do much more than you could do in straight Node. It does, however, provide cleaner structure for the code. There's also a beautifully simple middleware implementation for things such as logging and authentication and authorization. Useful for apps, it also has simple tools to serialize/deserialize JSON.

That's about it, though—it's a simple web framework that leaves most of the implementation up to you to decide.

DATABASES FOR NODE.JS

Since Node.js is written in JavaScript, it supports JSON in a very clean way. Manipulating JSON data is easy, which is great since that's what clients typically use.

On the back end, SQL databases are not a great fit for Node.js. Object-relational mappers (ORMs, which are the tools that connect your code to a relational database) and other tools out there are really young, and not a lot of work is currently being done to develop them. I doubt Node.js will ever have a great ORM. Having said that, it's common to see applications that use Node.js as a layer to an MVC web server that has a solid ORM.

That's okay, though, because there are great document databases out now such as Riak, MongoDB, RethinkDB, and Cassandra. JSON is a good fit for all of these since it represents a document naturally. Some databases, like MongoDB, use a JSON superset as their own internal storage engine.

Because MongoDB is by far the most common choice for Node.js applications, that's what you will be looking at in this book.

WHAT IS MongoDB?

To complete the JavaScript web stack, you will be using a document database called MongoDB. It has a number of advantages over a traditional SQL database. Since almost all developers know SQL already, I'm assuming you do as well. If you don't, don't worry if the SQL bits are over your head here; you don't need to worry about them. SQL is extremely complex and takes decades to master. MongoDB is simple and can be learned in an afternoon.

Having said that, I have found that learning MongoDB is a bit tricky for those who already know SQL. The more SQL you know, the harder it is to wrap your head around MongoDB; it's a different way of thinking. If this applies to you, my advice is to attempt to clear your head and not think about what you know about databases. MongoDB is more akin to working with objects in a programming language than what you know of as a database. Also, you're going to be breaking a lot of SQL rules, so be prepared to be a bit scared.

DOCUMENT-ORIENTED

Rather than storing data in a series of rows and tables like in SQL, MongoDB has *collections* and *documents*. While you can mostly think of a collection being like a table, a document is quite a bit different from a row.

The main reason documents are different is that they can contain way more information. In SQL, if you wanted to represent a user and their roles, you might have three tables for the task, as shown here:

USERS	
user_id	email
100	jeff@dickeyxxx.com
101	bob@dickeyxxx.com

ROLES	
role_id	name
1	Admin
2	Operations

USER_ROLES	
role_id	user_id
1	101
1	102
2	102

Finding out what user is in what role is a process of joining users across the user_roles table to the roles table. It's the way databases have been built forever.

In MongoDB, this is all much simpler. More than likely, you would have documents that look like the following:

```
{
  "_id" : ObjectId("538c997dac697631f0dfebce"),
  "email" : "jeff@dickey.xxx",
  "roles" : [ "admin", "operations" ]
}
```

In MongoDB this would be the only item in the database to represent the same data. If you come from the SQL world, there's a chance you may look at this and be a bit worried about the data duplication of having a different string for each role, for each user. "What if you wanted to change *admin* to *administrator*?" might be a question you would ask.

This is a trade-off you take in MongoDB. In SQL, the goal with the data is to structure it so that it is as normalized as possible with no duplicated information. In MongoDB you have a much different goal: to make the data as easy for the application to use as possible. While it might be more work to rename a role (you'd have to iterate over every user), that is a choice you make because it would be a relatively uncommon task. Finding out the roles a user is in, however, is much more common and easy in MongoDB. Querying for a user would just return the roles along with all the other information.

Not only is this querying easier as a developer, it's also much faster under the hood. This format is known as BSON.

BSON

MongoDB stores the data into a format called BSON, which is essentially just JSON stored as binary with a few differences. One of the differences is the ObjectId value. This is a data type used in Mongo to uniquely identify documents. It is created automatically on each document (it's analogous to a primary key).

Since the ObjectId is a large pseudorandom number, you are unlikely to run into a situation where you generate two that are the same. For nearly all practical purposes, you can assume they will always be unique, which can be really handy. The only situation you would have to worry about a collision is if you were generating a large number in a short period of time. Even then, however, you'd have to be generating them so fast the database would be unlikely to keep up anyway. It's safe to assume they're always unique.

One of the cool things about ObjectId is that you can take an ObjectId and find out when it was created. (They're partially based on a timestamp.) Here's a tool that can find out when 538c997dac697631f0dfebce was made: *http://steveridout.github.io/ mongo-object-time/*.

The following are advantages of BSON over tables/rows:

- Documents map naturally to objects in programming languages.
- Embedded documents and arrays prevent the need for joins.
- Polymorphism is much easier since there is no schema.

HORIZONTAL SCALING WITH AUTO-SHARDING

While MongoDB was certainly designed with developer ease of use in mind, it's also great for scaling. MongoDB supports *horizontal scaling*, which is the ability to add more machines to a cluster to scale it. This is in contrast to *vertical scaling*, which is the idea that you scale up by increasing the horsepower of a single box.

Essentially with MongoDB you can just add boxes to your cluster to scale up for traffic.

In a relational database such as MySQL or PostgreSQL, you have limited options to increase the database performance. Once a database starts to get hit hard and you've upgraded the box to be as powerful as possible, you have few options to increase performance. You can analyze queries and attempt to optimize them, add more caching, move the data to other sources, and decrease query usage, but all of these tasks require lots of developer time to analyze and fix.

As a last resort, some relational database admins will resort to *sharding* the system. Sharding involves splitting the data across multiple databases. On a relational database, this is incredibly challenging and involves a ton of changes to the application to support it. Once sharding has been implemented, you lose the ability to perform many types of queries (anything across the whole data set).

MongoDB, on the other hand, embraces sharding. It assumes your data will be sharded from the beginning; therefore, queries like joins that would require the whole dataset are not supported at all. You're expected to design your system to support this architecture.

Having said that, MongoDB can't scale in this way forever. You'll be able to add a few databases to the system, but at some point it'll be too much work for them to all get quorum with each other, and your system will break down. It's a good solution, but it isn't a silver bullet.

SCHEMALESS

In SQL, you have to design your schema by defining all the tables and data types before you can start inserting it. MongoDB does not have this concept. In MongoDB, you just start adding data in any format you want. If it doesn't look like earlier data, it doesn't complain.

In general, with MongoDB you don't set up anything beforehand; you just start using it. For example, there's no command to create an index. There *is* an ensureIndex command that does exactly what it sounds like (create the index if it doesn't exist).

INSTALLING MongoDB

Follow the directions for your platform at *http://docs.mongodb.org/manual/installation/*.

- On OS X with Homebrew, use `brew install mongodb`.
- Note that on OS X you'll probably want to make sure it stays running as a daemon with `launchctl`. Type `brew info mongodb` for instructions on how to do this.
- On Windows there is an installer you can get from the official website.
- On Ubuntu do *not* simply run `apt-get` because you will likely install a very old version of mongodb. Check the official website for specific instructions.

USING MongoDB

Now that you have MongoDB installed, start the `mongod` daemon and then start your client by running the `mongo` command:

```
$ mongo
MongoDB shell version: 2.6.1
connecting to: test
> _
```

Now you're connected to the `test` database. In MongoDB there are three parts to the hierarchy of data:

- **Database**: There is usually one database per app, but there can be several per server. It usually shares the name of the app, and it's the same as a database in SQL.
- **Collection**: This is a group of similar pieces of data. It is usually a noun and is analogous to a table in SQL.
- **Document**: This is a single item in the database, such as an individual user record. If a collection were a class, a document would be an object. It is sort of analogous to a row in SQL (although you shouldn't assume so!).

Here you want to use a database called `playground`. As mentioned earlier, in Mongo typically you won't create anything; you just start using it as if it was there. This is a great example:

```
> use playground
switched to db playground
> _
```

INSERTING DOCUMENTS

Now you can add your first document to a new collection called users.

```
> db.users.insert({name: 'Jeff Dickey', email: 'jeff@dickeyxxx.com',
  roles: ['admin', 'operations']})
WriteResult({ "nInserted" : 1 })
> _
```

QUERYING DOCUMENTS

Now that you've written your first document to the database, you can retrieve it with the find command.

```
db.users.find()
{ "_id" : ObjectId("538fd19837651880ee24565f"), "name" : "Jeff Dickey",
  "email" : "jeff@dickeyxxx.com", "roles" : [ "admin", "operations" ] }
> _
```

Most of the data there is exactly what you had before, except MongoDB has added an ObjectID attribute for you to uniquely identify this record across an entire database. You can get back a single record like this:

```
> db.users.find(ObjectId("538fd19837651880ee24565f"))
```

Or if you wanted to look up by e-mail, you'd use this:

```
> db.users.find({email: 'jeff@dickeyxxx.com'})
```

And by role, you'd use this:

```
> db.users.find({roles: 'admin'})
```

Searching inside an array assumes you're matching any one of the items in the array unless you pass an array in the query.

NOTE: In case you haven't noticed, the query language here is JavaScript. Even in the most raw database forms of the MEAN stack, you use JavaScript.

## CHAPTER 3

Introducing the Social Networking Project

Now that I've introduced the components of a MEAN application, in this chapter you will use those components to build a practical application.

The application will look similar to Twitter. There will be a main page showing the newest posts, and there will be a profile page for each user showing their recent posts. As you explore different parts of the application, I'll introduce new features such as live updating via WebSockets.

To start, you'll build a page showing the most recent posts. Posts will be anonymous until you add some authentication.

CREATING A STATIC MOCKUP OF THE RECENT POSTS PAGE

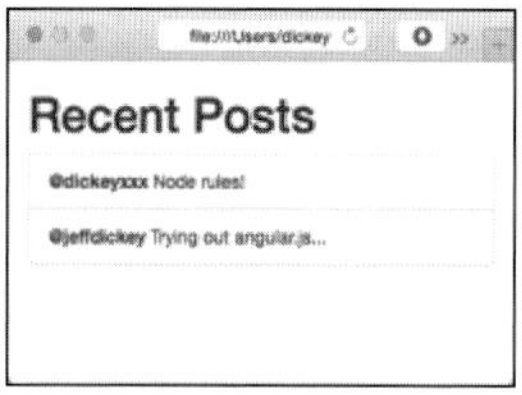

FIGURE 3.1 Recent
Posts page

The first step is to build a static mockup page with HTML and Bootstrap (*http://getbootstrap.com*)
for styling. Create a new directory for your application and create a file called posts.html with
the following HTML:

```
<!DOCTYPE html>
<html>
<head>
  <link rel="stylesheet" href="http://netdna.bootstrapcdn.com/bootstrap/3.1.1/
  → css/bootstrap.min.css">
</head>
<body>
  <div class='container'>
    <h1>Recent Posts</h1>
    <ul class='list-group'>
      <li class='list-group-item'>
        <strong>@dickeyxxx</strong>
        <span>Node rules!</span>
      </li>
      <li class='list-group-item'>
        <strong>@jeffdickey</strong>
        <span>Trying out angular.js...</span>
      </li>
    </ul>
  </div>
</body>
</html>
```

Now open this HTML document in your browser. You should see the screen shown
in **Figure 3.1**. I like to start building all Angular features following this approach, first by
dropping static HTML into a page and then replicating it with dynamic Angular code.

ANGULARIZING THE PAGE

Angular.js essentially allows you to data bind JavaScript objects to the DOM (also known as HTML elements). You basically wire up objects in a controller to something called $scope and declare in your HTML how it should be displayed.

Include Angular before your closing </body> tag:

```
<script src='https://ajax.googleapis.com/ajax/libs/angularjs/1.2.18/
→ angular.js'></script>
```

Now declare your <body> element as an Angular app:

```
<body ng-app='app'>
```

For this to work, you need to first declare a matching module. Do the following in a <script> tag after the Angular include tag:

```
<script>
  angular.module('app', [])
</script>
```

At this part of the book, you will be working in a <script> tag inside the HTML rather than referencing external JavaScript files. It might seem messy, but this is just temporary until you get Node to serve your HTML for you.

Modules are a way to separate parts of Angular code. This is a module declaration; the first argument is the name of the module, and the second is an array of modules that this module depends on. You'll use modules to get access to things such as ngAnimate (animation tools), ngRoute (client-side router for single-page apps), or modules of your own. I'll talk more about modules later, but for now just know that your app must be declared as a module.

To declare a controller, you call the .controller() method on an instance of a module. This method takes two arguments: a name and a function used to build an instance of the controller. All Angular components follow this same pattern.

Make your <script> tag look like the following:

```
<script>
  var app = angular.module('app', [])
  app.controller('PostsCtrl', function ($scope) {
    $scope.posts = [
      {
        username: 'dickeyxxx',
        body: 'Node rules!'
      },
      {
        username: 'jeffdickey',
```

```
        body: 'trying out angular.js...'
      }
    ]
  })
</script>
```

Here you're storing the app module into a variable app and then creating a controller on it called PostsCtrl. This controller has an array that represents the posts you see in the HTML.

When you declare a controller, you do what's known in the Angular world as *dependency inject $scope.*

Creating a controller (or other Angular component) involves declaring a function like you did earlier. When you declare arguments, Angular looks up the dependencies based on what you named them. If you rename $scope to $foobar, for example, you would see an error (although not with the code you have right now since the controller wouldn't load). In my opinion, this dependency injection is the most powerful part of Angular.

What is $scope? It's simply an object you can access in the HTML and in the controller.

You'll see more examples of dependencies later. For now, let's just dump $scope.posts onto the page. Add the following HTML to the page (keep your existing static HTML mockup for reference):

```
<div ng-controller='PostsCtrl'>
  {{ posts }}
</div>
```

You should now see a JSON representation of the controller's $scope.posts on the page. You can have JavaScript inside those double-curly brackets, so if you wanted to see just the body of the first post, you would do this:

```
<div ng-controller='PostsCtrl'>
  {{ posts[0].body }}
</div>
```

Remember that when sharing controller data to the view, use $scope. When referencing controller data from the view, leave *out* $scope.

Now that you're this far, you can finish Angularizing this page, at least the static version of it. Here's a complete example:

```html
<!DOCTYPE html>
<html>
<head>
  <link rel="stylesheet" href="http://netdna.bootstrapcdn.com/bootstrap/3.1.1/
  ↪ css/bootstrap.min.css">
</head>
<body ng-app='app'>
  <div ng-controller='PostsCtrl' class='container'>
    <h1>Recent Posts</h1>
    <ul class='list-group'>
      <li ng-repeat='post in posts' class='list-group-item'>
        <strong>@{{ post.username }}</strong>
        <span>{{ post.body }}</span>
      </li>
    </ul>
  </div>
  <script src='https://ajax.googleapis.com/ajax/libs/angularjs/1.2.18/
  ↪ angular.js'></script>
  <script>
    var app = angular.module('app', [])
    app.controller('PostsCtrl', function ($scope) {
      $scope.posts = [
        {
          username: 'dickeyxxx',
          body: 'Node rules!'
        },
        {
          username: 'jeffdickey',
          body: 'trying out angular.js...'
        }
      ]
    })
  </script>
</body>
</html>
```

ADDING NEW POSTS

FIGURE 3.2 Angular-ized Recent Posts page

You've now linked up the code to Angular such that your controller is providing the data and then allowing the view to display it, but right now it's the same as when you started with the static HTML.

What you need to do is have a field on the page for users to add new posts.

If you add a new element to the $scope.posts array, Angular will automatically update the view to show it. If you also have an input and button on the page to add a new post, you just need to append to that array.

To illustrate, let's add a button to the page. Before the list-group <ul>, add this button:

```
<button ng-click='addPost()' class='btn btn-default'>Add Post</button>
```

ng-click is a directive that is typically used to call a function on $scope. Right now clicking it will do nothing, but if you add the function, you can add a new post to your list of posts. Add the following line inside your controller:

```
$scope.addPost = function () {
  $scope.posts.unshift({
    username: 'dickeyxxx',
    body: 'my new post!'
  })
}
```

unshift is a JavaScript method on arrays that pushes a new element to the beginning of the array. You should now be able to click the Add Post button and add elements to the list (see **Figure 3.2**).

Because you didn't have to write any code to actually update the list when $scope.posts changed, this allows you to cleanly separate the logic that updates the data from the view logic. If you updated the posts by deletion, Ajax call, or WebSockets information, you just need to update $scope.posts, and Angular will take care of updating the view for you.

Now you need to add a couple of inputs to let the user put their own body in as the post. To do this, you will add an <input> to the page, data bind it to $scope, and then use that under addPost(). Add the following HTML before the Add Post button:

```
<input ng-model='postBody' class='form-control' />
```

The ng-model directive hooks an input to a $scope property. Now if you access $scope.postBody inside the controller, you'll get the data inside this text field.

To use this instead of your stock data, update the addPost() function like so:

```
$scope.addPost = function () {
  $scope.posts.unshift({
    username: 'dickeyxxx',
    body: $scope.postBody
  })
}
```

Now whatever the user enters in the input field will be their post body.

One issue is that the field doesn't clear after they make a post. To fix that, simply set $scope.postBody to null inside addPost():

```
$scope.postBody = null
```

Because the data binding is two-way, anything you set $scope.postBody to will update the input element, and vice versa.

Another issue is that the user can post empty posts. To fix that, simply wrap the addPost() logic in the following conditional:

```
if ($scope.postBody) {
```

Here is a complete example of the app with some Bootstrap code added for pizazz:

```
<!DOCTYPE html>
<html>
<head>
  <link rel="stylesheet" href="http://netdna.bootstrapcdn.com/bootstrap/3.1.1/
  → css/bootstrap.min.css">
</head>
<body ng-app='app'>
  <div ng-controller='PostsCtrl' class='container'>
    <h1>Recent Posts</h1>
    <form role='form'>
      <div class='form-group'>
```

```html
      <div class='input-group'>
        <input ng-model='postBody' class='form-control' />
        <span class='input-group-btn'>
          <button ng-click='addPost()' class='btn btn-default'>
          → Add Post</button>
        </span>
      </div>
    </div>
  </form>
  <ul class='list-group'>
    <li ng-repeat='post in posts' class='list-group-item'>
      <strong>@{{ post.username }}</strong>
      <span>{{ post.body }}</span>
    </li>
  </ul>
</div>
<script src='https://ajax.googleapis.com/ajax/libs/angularjs/1.2.18/
→ angular.js'></script>
<script>
  // create our app module
  var app = angular.module('app', [])

  // create the PostsCtrl module
  // dependency inject $scope
  app.controller('PostsCtrl', function ($scope) {

    // the function runs when the "Add Post" button is clicked
    $scope.addPost = function () {
      // Only add a post if there is a body
      if ($scope.postBody) {
        // unshift a new post into $scope.posts
        $scope.posts.unshift({
          username: 'dickeyxxx',
          body: $scope.postBody // use the text entered
        })
        // clear out the input field
        $scope.postBody = null
      }
    }
```

```
      // starting data
      $scope.posts = [
        {
          username: 'dickeyxxx',
          body: 'Node rules!'
        },
        {
          username: 'jeffdickey',
          body: 'trying out angular.js...'
        }
      ]
    })
  </script>
</body>
</html>
```

NEXT STEPS

You now have a fully functioning app for posting status updates. As I'm sure you're astutely aware, the major problem now is that it never persists. These posts disappear when the user closes the browser window. You could persist them into the browser's local storage, but that wouldn't allow you to share the data with other users (which is pretty important for a social networking application).

In the next chapter, you'll build an API for this application to persist the posts. Then in Chapter 5, you'll integrate this Angular app with the Node API you've built.

CHAPTER 4

Building a
Node.js API

In the previous chapter, you built a fully functioning Angular app for posting status updates. In this chapter, you will build an API for it to get a list of all the posts and to make a new post. The endpoints will be as follows:

- GET /api/posts returns a JSON array of all the posts. This is similar to what you had in $scope.posts.
- POST /api/posts expects a JSON document containing a username and post body. It will save that post in MongoDB.

THE STOCK ENDPOINT

To start, you'll use Node.js and Express to build a stock /api/posts endpoint. First, inside a new folder, create a package.json file like the following:

```
{
  "name": "socialapp"
}
```

The name can be anything you want, but try to ensure it doesn't conflict with an existing package. The package.json file is the only thing you need to make a directory a node project.

Now that you have this, you can add express and body-parser as dependencies:

```
$ cd <path-to-project-folder>
$ npm install --save express
$ npm install --save body-parser
```

body-parser is used for express to read in JSON on POST requests automatically.

The --save flag saves the dependency to the package.json file so you know what versions of what packages the app was built with (and therefore depends on). In fact, if you open your package.json, you'll see something similar to this:

```
{
  "name": "socialapp",
  "dependencies": {
    "body-parser": "^1.4.3",
    "express": "^4.4.4"
  }
}
```

Now that you've done this, you can require('express') to include it in a node script.

Create a `server.js` file with the following contents:

```
var express = require('express')
var bodyParser = require('body-parser')

var app = express()
app.use(bodyParser.json())

app.get('/api/posts', function (req, res) {
  res.json([
    {
      username: 'dickeyxxx',
      body: 'node rocks!'
    }
  ])
})

app.listen(3000, function () {
  console.log('Server listening on', 3000)
})
```

Try running this file:

```
$ node server.js
```

You can access it in your browser at *http://localhost:3000/api/posts*. You should see that your stubbed JSON comes back.

You now have the basic Node request in place, so you need to add the POST endpoint for adding posts and back it against MongoDB.

CREATING POSTS VIA THE API

Now let's build the POST endpoint for creating posts. Add this endpoint to server.js:

```
app.post('/api/posts', function (req, res) {
  console.log('post received!')
  console.log(req.body.username)
  console.log(req.body.body)
  res.send(201)
})
```

This is just a request that checks to see whether you're reading the data properly. The client would receive only the HTTP status code 201 (created). It's good to build a lot of these stubbed-out sorts of logic to check to see whether your plumbing is in order when building MEAN applications. Because you can't test a POST request using the browser, you should check to see whether it is working using curl:

```
curl -v -H "Content-Type: application/json" -XPOST --data
→ "{\"username\":\"dickeyxxx\", \"body\":\"node rules!\"}"
→ localhost:3000/api/posts
```

If you are unfamiliar with curl, this says "Make a POST request to *localhost:3000/api/posts*. Be verbose." Setting your Content-Type header to json includes the JSON document as the body.

The Content-Type header is necessary to be able to parse this content into the friendly req.body.username objects from the JSON.

If the command line isn't your thing, you can do this same thing using the great Postman app for Chrome to test APIs. Regardless of what method you use, it is crucial you test your APIs using stub clients like this rather than building your app in lockstep.

MongoDB MODELS WITH MONGOOSE

To interact with MongoDB, you will be using the Mongoose ODM. It's a light layer on top of the Mongo driver. To add the npm package, do this:

```
$ npm install --save mongoose
```

It'll be good to keep this code modularized so your server.js file doesn't get huge. Let's add a db.js file with some of the base database connection logic:

```
var mongoose = require('mongoose')
mongoose.connect('mongodb://localhost/social', function () {
  console.log('mongodb connected')
})
module.exports = mongoose
```

You can get access to this mongoose instance by using the require function. Now let's create a mongoose model to store the posts. Place this code in models/post.js:

```
var db = require('../db')
var Post = db.model('Post', {
  username: { type: String, required: true },
  body:     { type: String, required: true },
  date:     { type: Date, required: true, default: Date.now }
})
module.exports = Post
```

Now you have a model you can get with require. You can use it to interact with the database.

USING MONGOOSE MODELS WITH THE POST ENDPOINT

Now requiring this module will give you the Post model, which you can use inside of your endpoint to create posts.

In server.js, change your app.post('/api/posts') endpoint to the following:

```
var Post = require('./models/post')
app.post('/api/posts', function (req, res, next) {
  var post = new Post({
    username: req.body.username,
    body: req.body.body
  })
  post.save(function (err, post) {
    if (err) { return next(err) }
    res.json(201, post)
  })
})
```

First, you require the Post model. When a request comes in, you build up a new instance of the Post model with new Post(). Then, you save that Post model and return a JSON representation of the model to the user with status code 201.

While it isn't totally necessary to return the JSON here, I like for my create API actions to do so. The client can sometimes make use of it. It might be able to use the _id field or show data that the server generated (such as the date field, for example).

Note the err line. In Node, it's common for code to return callbacks like this that start with an error argument, and then the data is returned. It's your responsibility to check whether there is an error message and do something about it. In this case, you call the next() callback with an argument, which triggers a 500 in Express. An error in this case would typically mean the database was having issues. Other programming languages use exceptions to handle errors like this, but Node.js made the design decision to go with error objects because of its asynchronous nature. It's simply not possible to bubble up an exception with evented code like Node.js.

Go ahead and hit this endpoint again with curl or Postman. (Make sure you first restart your server. Later you'll see how to automatically restart it with nodemon.)

```
$ curl -v -H "Content-Type: application/json" -XPOST --data
→ "{\"username\":\"dickeyxxx\", \"body\":\"node rules!\"}"
→ localhost:3000/api/posts
```

You should see a response like the following (make sure you've started your Mongo server):

```
> POST /api/posts HTTP/1.1
> User-Agent: curl/7.30.0
> Host: localhost:3000
> Accept: */*
> Content-Type: application/json
> Content-Length: 46
>
* upload completely sent off: 46 out of 46 bytes
< HTTP/1.1 201 Created
< X-Powered-By: Express
< Content-Type: application/json; charset=utf-8
< Content-Length: 120
< Date: Sun, 22 Jun 2014 00:41:55 GMT
< Connection: keep-alive
<
* Connection #0 to host localhost left intact
{"__v":0,"username":"dickeyxxx","body":"node rules!","_id":
→ "53a62653fa305e5ddb318c1b","date":"2014-06-22T00:41:55.040Z"}
```

Since you see an _id field coming back, I'm pretty sure it's working. Just to be sure, though, let's check the database directly with the mongo command:

```
$ mongo social
MongoDB shell version: 2.6.1
connecting to social
> db.posts.find()
{ "_id" : ObjectId("53a62653fa305e5ddb318c1b"), "username" : "dickeyxxx",
→ "body" : "node rules!", "date" : ISODate("2014-06-22T00:41:55.040Z"),
→ "__v" : 0 }
```

Looks like it made it into the database!

Now, let's update the GET request to read from the database:

```
app.get('/api/posts', function (req, res, next) {
  Post.find(function(err, posts) {
    if (err) { return next(err) }
    res.json(posts)
  })
})
```

This one is similar to the last one. Call `find` on the `Post` model; then, when the request returns, render out the posts as JSON (so long as no error was returned). Go back to your web browser and reload *http://localhost:3000/api/posts* to see it in action.

You now have a full API you can read and write from in order to support your Angular app. Here is the final `server.js`:

```
var express = require('express')
var bodyParser = require('body-parser')
var Post = require('./models/post')

var app = express()
app.use(bodyParser.json())

app.get('/api/posts', function (req, res, next) {
  Post.find(function(err, posts) {
    if (err) { return next(err) }
    res.json(posts)
  })
})

app.post('/api/posts', function (req, res, next) {
  var post = new Post({
    username: req.body.username,
    body: req.body.body
  })
  post.save(function (err, post) {
    if (err) { return next(err) }
    res.json(201, post)
  })
})

app.listen(3000, function () {
  console.log('Server listening on', 3000)
})
```

NEXT STEPS

You've now built the full API for you to use with the Angular app. In the next chapter, you'll integrate the API into Angular and serve the Angular app via Node. You'll also take some time to clean up your code a little by breaking it into modules.

## CHAPTER 5

Integrating Node with Angular

Now that you've built your API, it's time to use it with Angular. Also, since Node is a web server, it'd be nice to get it to serve your HTML rather than load it as a flat file like you've been doing thus far.

$HTTP

To perform HTTP calls in Angular, you'll use its built-in HTTP client: $http. If you haven't noticed yet, official Angular components start with $. You should not prefix components you create with a $.

$http is a pretty standard HTTP client with some of the usual suspects: $http.get(), $http.post(), and so on. It is *promise* based.

WHAT ARE PROMISES?

Promises are a way of writing asynchronous code in JavaScript as an alternative to the traditional callback method that Node uses.

If you look at a popular Node HTTP client, request, you can see the difference.

Here's Angular's $http:

```
$http.get('http://localhost:3000/api/posts')
.success(function (posts) {
  // do stuff with posts
})
.error(function (err) {
  // handle the error case (if you care)
})
```

And here's Node's request:

```
request.get('http://localhost:3000/api/posts', function (err, response, data) {
  if (err) { /* handle error */ }
  // do something with posts
})
```

The main difference here is that with promises, you get back an object that you can call methods on to give it different functions based on success/failure. In the callback method, there is just one function that has to handle every case.

It's not super important to understand promises in detail just yet, but do understand that Angular code is heavily promise based, and Node (conventionally) is not.

There is some controversy over which method is better. Promises have been definitely more popular recently and will be included in the next version of JavaScript (ES6). Some people use promises exclusively in Node, and you can do that in your own code if you want. In this book, I will use callbacks with Node code and promises with Angular code to fit the current conventions.

READING POSTS FROM THE API WITH $HTTP

If you go back to the Angular app (posts.html) and look at your controller, this is what you'll see:

```
app.controller('PostsCtrl', function ($scope) {
  $scope.addPost = function () {
    if ($scope.postBody) {
      $scope.posts.unshift({
        username: 'dickeyxxx',
        body: $scope.postBody
      })
    $scope.postBody = null
    }
  }
  $scope.posts = [
      {
        username: 'dickeyxxx',
        body: 'Node rules!'
      },
      {
        username: 'jeffdickey',
        body: 'trying out angular.js...'
      }
    ]
})
```

What you want to do is replace the $scope.posts array with an array you get from the API via $http. To start, first dependency inject $http when you create your controller:

```
app.controller('PostsCtrl', function ($scope, $http)
```

Now Angular will give you an instance of $http inside your controller. Replace the $scope.posts lines with the following:

```
$http.get('http://localhost:3000/api/posts')
.success(function (posts) {
  $scope.posts = posts
})
```

Note that you don't have to handle the error case of the API if you don't want to (one advantage of promises).

This should work in your Angular app, but there's a chance you may hit a CORS (cross-origin resource sharing) security issue. CORS is a security policy that browsers follow, instructing them to request data only from the same hostname the HTML is served from. There are ways to prevent this, but the best way for a MEAN app to do this is to serve `posts.html` from the API server.

This is a good idea for a lot of reasons; namely, it will allow you to use `/api/posts` instead of `http://localhost:3000/api/posts` in the Angular controller.

SERVING POSTS.HTML THROUGH NODE

To get Node hosting your HTML page, first copy your posts.html file into the Node app, under a new folder called /layouts. Why /layouts instead of something like /views or /templates? It's because later you'll have Angular partials that will go into a templates folder, and this will allow you to easily differentiate the full HTML pages from the partials.

Now open your server.js file and add the following endpoint:

```
app.get('/', function (req, res) {
  res.sendfile('layouts/posts.html')
})
```

Now after starting your Node app, open *http://localhost:3000* in your browser, and your app should be up!

If you are tired of restarting your node server all the time, I suggest using the nodemon package. It will automatically restart your node app if any files change.

```
$ npm install --global nodemon
$ nodemon server.js
```

SAVING POSTS TO THE API WITH $HTTP

Now that you can cleanly read the data from the API, you need to POST to the API when you add a new post. This will use $http as well. Edit the addPost() method in the Angular layout file to look like the following:

```
$scope.addPost = function () {
  if ($scope.postBody) {
    $http.post('/api/posts', {
      username: 'dickeyxxx',
      body: $scope.postBody
    }).success(function (post) {
      $scope.posts.unshift(post)
      $scope.postBody = null
    })
  }
}
```

What you're doing with this is sending the post to the server, and if it responds with a success status code, you unshift the new post onto $scope.posts.

You might note that it's totally possible to add it to the list *before* it finishes sending to the server. This would offer the illusion to the user that it posted much faster. This is one of the great things about having a thick client.

If you were to do this, it would be prudent to add an error function to the $http promise to remove it if it was unsuccessful.

If you add a couple posts and then refresh the page, you might notice a bug! Using unshift, new posts are correctly added to the top, but Node is returning the results in chronological order, not reverse chronological order as you'd expect.

FIXING THE POST ORDERING

Fixing the posts to be in reverse chronological order could be done either in the Node server or in Angular (or better yet, both). To do it in Angular, you simply add an orderBy predicate to the ng-repeat directive in /layouts/posts.html:

```
<li ng-repeat="post in posts | orderBy:'-date'" class='list-group-item'>
```

Angular will now correctly order the posts by the date you added to your Mongoose schema. Note that aside from adding it to the model schema, you didn't have to write any code to support dates. This demonstrates the power of using a MEAN stack. You can just add something to MongoDB, and it will cascade all the way to the client.

Alternatively, you can also sort this out in Node. This is a good idea to do if you wanted to add pagination to your API. You would want to make sure the first page of the response contained the newest posts. You won't be building the pagination just yet, but here is how you can edit server.js to serve the posts in reverse chronological order:

```
app.get('/api/posts', function (req, res, next) {
  Post.find()
  .sort('-date')
  .exec(function(err, posts) {
    if (err) { return next(err) }
    res.json(posts)
  })
})
```

Mongoose allows you to keep chaining the query with various methods like this. This could be useful for filtering out posts, for example.

CLEANING UP SERVER.JS

Now that your app is a little more fleshed out, the `server.js` file has started to reach out into too many things (setting up the server and adding the middleware, all of the API endpoints, and the bit that delivers the layout file). When building JavaScript applications, there is a lot of flexibility you get in how to structure the codebase. It's best to start simple with few files so you can quickly iterate on them. When files start to get large, there comes a time when you'll want to break them out.

Here is the current `server.js` file:

```
var express = require('express')
var bodyParser = require('body-parser')
var Post = require('./models/post')

var app = express()
app.use(bodyParser.json())

app.get('/api/posts', function (req, res, next) {
  Post.find()
  .sort('-date')
  .exec(function(err, posts) {
    if (err) { return next(err) }
    res.json(posts)
  })
})

app.post('/api/posts', function (req, res, next) {
  var post = new Post({
    username: req.body.username,
    body: req.body.body
  })
  post.save(function (err, post) {
    if (err) { return next(err) }
    res.json(201, post)
  })
})
```

```javascript
app.get('/', function (req, res) {
  res.sendfile('layouts/posts.html')
})

app.listen(3000, function () {
  console.log('Server listening on', 3000)
})
```

What I'd like to do now is to break out the API and sendfile endpoints into controllers.

BREAKING OUT /API/POSTS

First create a file /controllers/api/posts.js with the same code with the GET and POST /api/posts endpoints.

```javascript
var Post = require('../../models/post')

app.get('/api/posts', function (req, res, next) {
  Post.find()
  .sort('-date')
  .exec(function(err, posts) {
    if (err) { return next(err) }
    res.json(posts)
  })
})

app.post('/api/posts', function (req, res, next) {
  var post = new Post({
    username: req.body.username,
    body: req.body.body
  })
  post.save(function (err, post) {
    if (err) { return next(err) }
    res.json(201, post)
  })
})
```

This won't work because you don't have reference to the app object. One solution would be to wrap the whole bit of code into a function that expects an app argument, like so:

```
var Post = require('../../models/post')

module.exports = function (app) {
  app.get('/api/posts', function (req, res, next) {
    Post.find()
    .sort('-date')
    .exec(function(err, posts) {
      if (err) { return next(err) }
      res.json(posts)
    })
  })

  app.post('/api/posts', function (req, res, next) {
    var post = new Post({
      username: req.body.username,
      body: req.body.body
    })
    post.save(function (err, post) {
      if (err) { return next(err) }
      res.json(201, post)
    })
  })
}
```

Then you could call it from server.js like so:

```
require('./controllers/api/posts')(app)
```

This is a fine solution that has a side benefit of allowing you to easily mock out the app object if you wanted to write a test. Still, Express offers a cleaner solution through its Router object. You can build up a Router object that acts like an app object and simply use it like middleware to attach it to your app. In /controllers/api/posts.js, it would look like this:

```
var Post = require('../../models/post')
var router = require('express').Router()

router.get('/api/posts', function (req, res, next) {
  Post.find()
  .sort('-date')
  .exec(function(err, posts) {
```

```
    if (err) { return next(err) }
    res.json(posts)
  })
})

router.post('/api/posts', function (req, res, next) {
  var post = new Post({
    username: req.body.username,
    body: req.body.body
  })
  post.save(function (err, post) {
    if (err) { return next(err) }
    res.json(201, post)
  })
})

module.exports = router
```

Then you can attach it to your app in `server.js` like so (make sure you remove the old endpoints from `server.js` as well):

```
app.use(require('./controllers/api/posts'))
```

This is my preferred method because it allows you to do clever things such as using middleware on only the API. It also prevents you from having to indent all of your code inside a function definition.

NAMESPACING ROUTERS

You can even namespace your routes by passing the namespace into the `.use()` method:

```
app.use('/api/posts', require('./controllers/api/posts'))
```

Then in the controller, leave out that part of the path:

```
router.get('/', function (req, res, next) {
// ...
router.post('/', function (req, res, next) {
// ...
```

You could even have an API controller mounted to /api that then mounts the api/posts controller to /posts on itself. That's a bit too modular for our app right now, but a large app might benefit from that.

Try this now by running the app. You should see no change.

BREAKING OUT THE SENDFILE ENDPOINT

Now that you've broken out part of the code, let's break out the section that delivers the Angular app. Create a file /controllers/static.js with the following:

```
var router = require('express').Router()

router.get('/', function (req, res) {
  res.sendfile('layouts/posts.html')
})

module.exports = router
```

Then use it in server.js. The entire server.js file should now look like this:

```
var express = require('express')
var bodyParser = require('body-parser')

var app = express()
app.use(bodyParser.json())

app.use('/api/posts', require('./controllers/api/posts'))
app.use( require('./controllers/static'))
// equivalent to: app.use('/', require('./controllers/static'))

app.listen(3000, function () {
  console.log('Server listening on', 3000)
})
```

Most Express apps have a single entry point like this to start an instance of the server. It's good to keep it as lightweight as possible. Good things to define in server.js include the following:

- Global middleware
- Global configuration
- Telling the server to listen
- Logger setup
- Error handling
- Mounting controllers

CLEANING UP ANGULAR

Now that your Node code is looking cleaner, you can turn your focus to the front end. It would be really nice if you had your JavaScript in a separate file instead of baked into your layout. It would also be nice if the controller performed the $http logic inside a service to separate concerns and allow reuse.

SERVING STATIC ASSETS

To deliver the JavaScript as a separate file, first break it out into a file called /assets/app.js. Include the JavaScript script from /layouts/posts.html (the comments that were previously included have been removed):

```
var app = angular.module('app', [])

app.controller('PostsCtrl', function ($scope, $http) {
  $scope.addPost = function () {
    if ($scope.postBody) {
      $http.post('/api/posts', {
        username: 'dickeyxxx',
        body: $scope.postBody
      }).success(function (post) {
        $scope.posts.unshift(post)
        $scope.postBody = null
      })
    }
  }

  $http.get('/api/posts').success(function (posts) {
    $scope.posts = posts
  })
})
```

Node is capable of delivering static JS and CSS files like this. Now in production, you might not want Node serving a lot of these files since it's not as good as a general web server like nginx or Apache. Still, it's a great way to deliver them in development mode.

I'll get into serving your application in production later, but I want you to have an idea of the direction we will go. Later, you'll put a CDN in front of your application that will cache the assets. For now, you'll continue to serve them from Node because it's easier to configure and has fewer moving parts.

Since it works the same in production as it does in development, you achieve something called *dev-prod parity*. Dev-prod parity is the idea that production should be as similar to development mode as possible in order to mitigate production-specific issues.

To do this, Express comes with built-in middleware to serve up the static assets. You can add it to /controllers/static.js along with your layout endpoint:

```
var express = require('express')
var router = express.Router()


router.use(express.static(__dirname + '/../assets'))
```

__dirname is a special Node variable that points to the current file's directory, /controllers in this case. You're going up from that directory so that you can serve the assets in /assets.

You could also use process.cwd(), which is the current working directory of the Node process, but that has a tendency to change depending on how you start the process. I prefer using __dirname instead of process.cwd() for all Node web servers.

Once you have that set up, try to access *http://localhost:3000/app.js*. You should see the raw JavaScript script you created. Then replace the old <script> tag in /layouts/posts.html with one that references the script from the server.

```
<script src='/app.js'></script>
```

Now you have a much cleaner separation between your HTML layout and your JavaScript code.

BREAKING ANGULAR INTO SERVICES

In addition to the clever data binding that Angular provides, it provides a solid framework for breaking up your code into logical sections. Services are one of the ways you can build a component for use in your application.

In Angular, controllers get created and destroyed every time they appear and disappear on a page. Services, on the other hand, are created only once when needed. If multiple other components want to use a service, Angular will efficiently reuse the same instance of the service.

You dependency inject services just like $scope or $http and call custom functions on them.

A clear code smell inside Angular apps would be having $http inside a controller. This makes the controller aware of too much and isn't good code separation. Now, when building your applications, I encourage you to first make the HTTP calls inside the controller and break it out once it is working. That's how I build applications, and similar to the server.js breakout you did earlier, it allows for easier iterating and experimenting.

Inside /assets/app.js, define the service on the app object. It doesn't matter if you do it before or after the controller. Angular will automatically figure out the order to load these things when it runs.

The service to make the HTTP looks like this:

```
app.service('PostsSvc', function ($http) {
  this.fetch = function () {
    return $http.get('/api/posts')
  }
})
```

Name the service PostsSvc and then dependency inject $http. You then define a function on the service called fetch that returns the $http promise for loading posts. Now dependency inject PostsSvc into the controller (replacing $http):

```
app.controller('PostsCtrl', function ($scope, PostsSvc) {
```

And replace the code that loads the posts with the following:

```
PostsSvc.fetch().success(function (posts) {
  $scope.posts = posts
})
```

It might not seem like a huge improvement just yet, but this allows you to consolidate all the logic in regard to reading posts into one place. In a typical app, this might involve pagination, caching, authorization, or even making multiple HTTP calls. It has a side benefit of making the code easy to test in isolation.

Make sure this code is still able to read the posts from the API and then add a .create(post) method to the service. The service should now look like the following:

```
app.service('PostsSvc', function ($http) {
  this.fetch = function () {
    return $http.get('/api/posts')
  }
  this.create = function (post) {
    return $http.post('/api/posts', post)
  }
})
```

Then use it in the controller:

```javascript
app.controller('PostsCtrl', function ($scope, PostsSvc) {
  $scope.addPost = function () {
    if ($scope.postBody) {
      PostsSvc.create({
        username: 'dickeyxxx',
        body: $scope.postBody
      }).success(function (post) {
        $scope.posts.unshift(post)
        $scope.postBody = null
      })
    }
  }

  PostsSvc.fetch().success(function (posts) {
    $scope.posts = posts
  })
})
```

Now you've successfully modularized your Angular code into logical sections. Using this pattern, it's easy to manage even large Angular codebases in a performant way.

NEXT STEPS

You've now fully integrated Angular and Node together and have a working first version of your application. In the next chapter, I'll introduce Gulp as a way to manage building your app's assets.

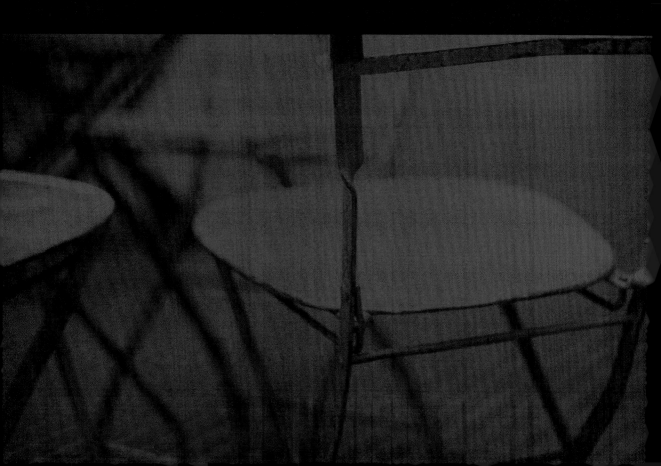

CHAPTER 6

Automating Your Build with Gulp

In the previous chapter, you learned how to integrate Angular with a Node API. In this chapter, you'll learn how to automate the build steps of your application with Gulp.

INTRODUCING GRUNT AND GULP

All modern JavaScript applications involve some kind of build process. This might entail preprocessing CSS with Sass/Less/Stylus, concatenating JavaScript files into one, minifying assets, compiling CoffeeScript, and so on. While this can totally be done with ad hoc commands or Bash scripts, there are tools that help you manage these tasks. Another benefit that is sometimes overlooked is these tools typically work on Windows machines and not just Mac and Linux boxes.

I highly encourage taking the time to learn a build tool. It will help clean up your build scripts, make it easier to work on projects you haven't touched in a while, and make it easier for others to work on your project.

A few tools can help with these tasks; the big two are Grunt and Gulp. Grunt is older than Gulp and is more task-centric. In Grunt, you define in JSON how to do things such as minify JavaScript and compile Sass, and each spits out a file. Gulp is stream-based, and the configuration is written in JavaScript code. Gulp configuration files are way shorter than the Grunt equivalent, and because of its streaming architecture Gulp will run orders of magnitude faster on large projects.

In my opinion, Gulp is a much better tool for asset build tasks and will be the tool used in this book.

GULP HELLO WORLD

To get Gulp up and running, let's first create a simple task that just outputs "Hello World." First, install Gulp globally and in the project (you need both) with the following commands:

```
npm install --global gulp
npm install --save gulp
```

Next, add the file gulpfile.js to the root of the project. This is a special filename Gulp knows to look for. The contents should be the following:

```
var gulp = require('gulp')

gulp.task('hello', function () {
  console.log('hello world')
})
```

You can now run this hello task:

```
$ gulp hello
[15:59:03] Using gulpfile ~/src/social/gulpfile.js
[15:59:03] Starting 'hello'...
hello world
[15:59:03] Finished 'hello' after 106 µs
```

This is the basic form of a Gulp task. You can also have tasks that depend on others by passing in an array:

```
var gulp = require('gulp')

gulp.task('welcome', function () {
  console.log('welcome to gulp!')
})

gulp.task('hello', ['welcome'], function () {
  console.log('hello world')
})
```

Now if you run the hello task, it will first wait for the welcome task to complete. You can also run the welcome task directly with gulp welcome.

BUILDING JAVASCRIPT WITH GULP

The first thing you will use Gulp to take care of is building your front-end JavaScript. Right now you have the /assets/app.js file that gets included inside the layout file, but I would like to have many JavaScript files to have a nice clean file hierarchy for all of your front-end code. Ideally, every Angular component would have its own file.

Having a <script> tag for each of these would quickly become unbearable, so what you'll do now is add a series of front-end scripts in /ng (for Angular) that Gulp will concatenate together to dynamically build /assets/app.js.

First, move /assets/app.js to /ng/app.js. Then, install the Gulp plug-in gulp-concat:

```
$ npm install --save gulp-concat
```

Replace your gulpfile.js file with the following:

```
var gulp = require('gulp')
var concat = require('gulp-concat')

gulp.task('js', function () {
  gulp.src('ng/**/*.js')
    .pipe(concat('app.js'))
    .pipe(gulp.dest('assets'))
})
```

This is the common signature of all Gulp plug-ins. You load the files with gulp.src into a stream, then pipe them through various plug-ins, and finally output them to gulp.dest. It might look a little unusual at first, but once you get the hang of it, you'll be able to use many plug-ins without even reading the documentation.

Try running gulp js, and you should see it copy the contents of /ng/app.js to /assets/app.js:

```
$ gulp js
```

Angular is great in that it allows you to declare the components at any time, so the order in which gulp-concat adds the files doesn't matter for the components. However, you do need access to the module object you create with angular.module('app', []).

angular.module() is a method that can be used as either a getter or a setter. If you pass in one argument (the name of the module), it will return that module (*getter*). If you pass in two arguments (name and dependencies), it is a *setter*. The *setter* can be called only once and *must* be called before any *getters*. This is an important note because it trips people up sometimes setting up the project.

The main point here is you have to call angular.module('app', []) once before any of your code; then you can call angular.module('app') in each component file to get back that instance.

Replace /ng/app.js with the following three files:

Here are the contents for the file /ng/module.js:

```
angular.module('app', [])
```

Here are the contents for the file /ng/posts.ctrl.js:

```
angular.module('app')
.controller('PostsCtrl', function ($scope, PostsSvc) {
  $scope.addPost = function () {
    if ($scope.postBody) {
      PostsSvc.create({
        username: 'dickeyxxx',
        body: $scope.postBody
      }).success(function (post) {
        $scope.posts.unshift(post)
        $scope.postBody = null
      })
    }
  }

  PostsSvc.fetch().success(function (posts) {
    $scope.posts = posts
  })
})
```

Here are the contents for the file /ng/posts.svc.js:

```
angular.module('app')
.service('PostsSvc', function ($http) {
  this.fetch = function () {
    return $http.get('/api/posts')
  }
  this.create = function (post) {
    return $http.post('/api/posts', post)
  }
})
```

Now you just need to make sure that concat loads /ng/module.js first before the other files. Replace the Gulp task with the following that does this:

```
gulp.task('js', function () {
  gulp.src(['ng/module.js', 'ng/**/*.js'])
    .pipe(concat('app.js'))
    .pipe(gulp.dest('assets'))
})
```

You now have a really simple process to import the module first, and you are free to add the Angular code to /ng in any place, and Gulp will automatically import the files.

If you're not using Angular and therefore aren't able to use its dependency injection, I suggest using Browserify to require JavaScript files instead of this method. You could use Browserify as well in this project, but it's totally overkill for Angular apps since all you need to do is define the module before anything else. If you're using source control, it's usually a good idea to ignore the assets folder. Checking the compiled assets into the project will make the repository grow quite large.

UGLIFIER

It'd be great to also minify your JavaScript code before you build /assets/app.js to reduce the file size when users download the application. Uglifier is a popular tool for JavaScript minification.

First install the Uglify plug-in:

```
$ npm install --save gulp-uglify
```

Modify your gulp task to use it:

```
var gulp = require('gulp')
var concat = require('gulp-concat')
var uglify = require('gulp-uglify')

gulp.task('js', function () {
  gulp.src(['ng/module.js', 'ng/**/*.js'])
    .pipe(concat('app.js'))
    .pipe(uglify())
    .pipe(gulp.dest('assets'))
})
```

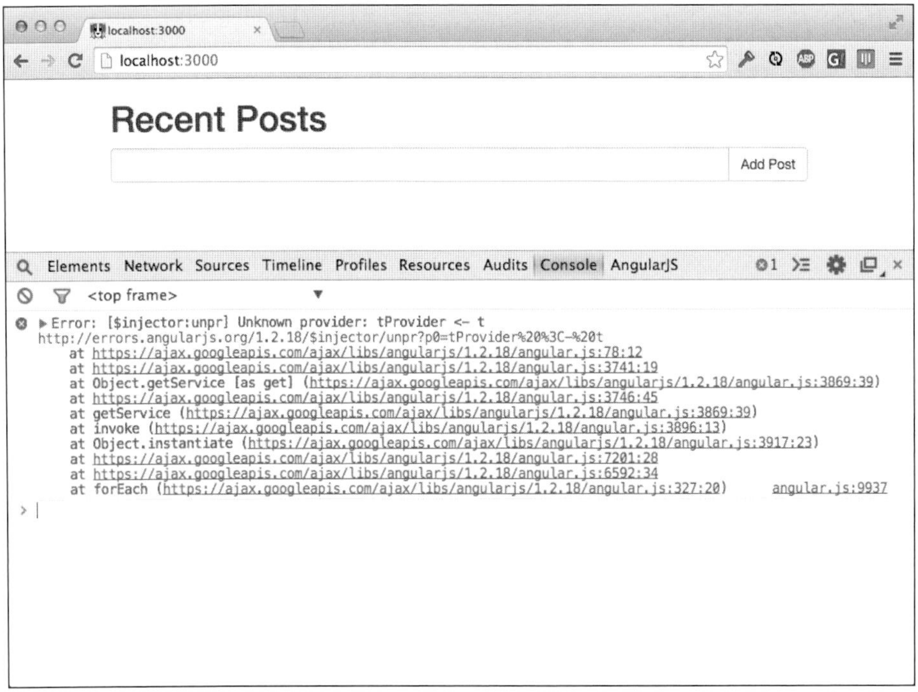

FIGURE 6.1 Error after including Uglifier

Now if you run the task and open /assets/app.js, you can clearly see it is now minified (note that Uglifier might not output code exactly like this on your machine):

```
angular.module("app",[]);
angular.module("app").controller("PostsCtrl",function(o,s)
→ {o.addPost=function(){o.postBody&&s.create({username:"dickeyxxx",
→ body:o.postBody}).success(function(s){o.posts.unshift(s),
→ o.postBody=null})},s.fetch().success(function(s){o.posts=s})});
angular.module("app").service("PostsSvc",function(t){this.fetch=function()
→ {return t.get("/api/posts")},this.create=function(s){return t.post
→ ("/api/posts",s)}});
```

However, if you run the application now, you get an error and nothing works (see **Figure 6.1**)!

That "Unknown provider" error is one you're likely to see in Angular development. It means that the dependency injector could not find a dependency. In this case, it was looking for the dependency o.

What is happening here is that Uglifier rewrote the function argument names as single characters. For this reason, Angular is incompatible with JavaScript minifiers. Obviously, there is a way to fix this problem. You can pass an array that defines the dependencies as strings when defining your component. For example, if you wanted to fix PostsSvc, you could change the definition from this:

```
.service('PostsSvc', function ($http) {
```

into this:

```
.service('PostsSvc', ['$http', function ($http) {
```

Angular supports either way to define the dependencies. The second one is minifier-compatible since the minifier won't change the string literal the way it changes variable names. While this is great for minification, it's a pain to develop with since you have to keep track of the order of dependencies all the time.

Luckily, there is a tool called ng-annotate that will rewrite your code using the minification-friendly syntax before you ship it off to Uglifier. This allows you to write the code in the concise manner and solves the minification problem as well. It's similar to other Gulp plug-ins.

First, install gulp-ng-annotate:

```
$ npm install --save gulp-ng-annotate
```

Then update your gulpfile.js:

```
var gulp = require('gulp')
var concat = require('gulp-concat')
var uglify = require('gulp-uglify')
var ngAnnotate = require('gulp-ng-annotate')

gulp.task('js', function () {
  gulp.src(['ng/module.js', 'ng/**/*.js'])
    .pipe(concat('app.js'))
    .pipe(ngAnnotate())
    .pipe(uglify())
    .pipe(gulp.dest('assets'))
})
```

Starting to see the Gulp pattern? Do an npm install, add the require(), and then add it into the pipe() sequence. Almost all Gulp plug-ins work like this.

Rebuilding /assets/app.js should now result in the following:

```
angular.module("app",[]);
angular.module("app").controller("PostsCtrl",["$scope","PostsSvc",function
→ (s,o){s.addPost=function(){s.postBody&&o.create({username:"dickeyxxx",
→ body:s.postBody}).success(function(o){s.posts.unshift(o),s.postBody=null})},
→ o.fetch().success(function(o){s.posts=o})}]);
angular.module("app").service("PostsSvc",["$http",function(t){this.fetch=
→ function(){return t.get("/api/posts")},this.create=function(s){return t.post
→ ("/api/posts",s)}}]);
```

If you look in there, you'll see how it added those dependency arrays to each component. Running the app again should now work.

REBUILDING UPON FILE CHANGES

Right now the Angular code is concatenated and minified by using gulp js, but it would be a huge pain to have to run that command every time you make a change. It's pretty easy to add a file watcher in Gulp that will automatically rebuild the JavaScript every time there is a change.

Here's a Gulp task that will rerun js every time one of the Angular files changes:

```
gulp.task('watch:js', ['js'], function () {
  gulp.watch('ng/**/*.js', ['js'])
})
```

gulp.watch takes in a file path to watch and then an array of tasks to run whenever those files are edited.

If you now run gulp watch:js instead of gulp js, it will stay up, rebuilding the JavaScript whenever a JavaScript file in /ng changes, just like nodemon will restart Node when server.js changes. Note that I also added the js task as a dependency. This way, when you first call watch:js, it will automatically build the JavaScript even before a file changes.

Having an easy setup like this is crucial. Your development environment needs to be seamless with as few chores to take care of as possible when building your application.

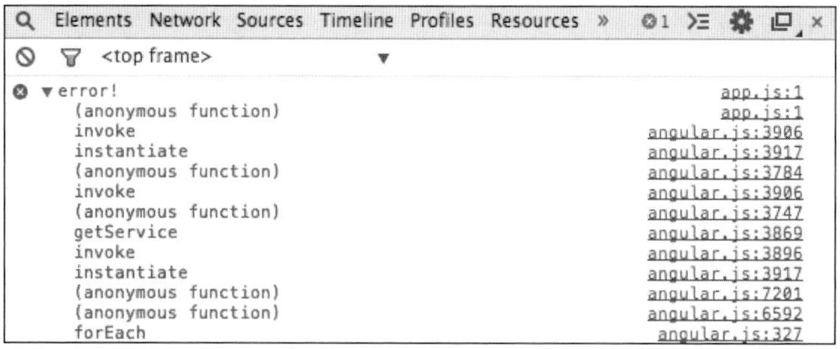

FIGURE 6.2 Logging an error without a source map

```
Q    Elements  Network  Sources  Timeline  Profiles  Resources  »    ⊘1  ≥≡  ⚙  ▢  ×
⊘    ▽   <top frame>                        ▼
⊗  ▼ error!                                                              app.js:1
        (anonymous function)                                            app.js:1
        invoke                                                   angular.js:3906
        instantiate                                             angular.js:3917
        (anonymous function)                                    angular.js:3784
        invoke                                                  angular.js:3906
        (anonymous function)                                    angular.js:3747
        getService                                              angular.js:3869
        invoke                                                  angular.js:3896
        instantiate                                             angular.js:3917
        (anonymous function)                                    angular.js:7201
        (anonymous function)                                    angular.js:6592
        forEach                                                  angular.js:327
```

SOURCE MAPS

Another issue with minification is that it makes it harder to debug the code. Now when the browser sees a console.log or error pop up, it can't easily tell you where the code caused a problem. Like having Gulp rebuild your code when it changes, this isn't necessary to build your application, but doing it will save you a lot of work in the future.

First, I'll demonstrate the problem. Add the line console.error('error!') inside PostsSvc (ng/posts.svc.js). If you're using Chrome, you should see output like that shown in **Figure 6.2** in the Developer Tools Console tab.

It is saying the error happened on line 3 of app.js, which is totally unhelpful because that's the minified code. By including a source map of the original JavaScript, you can provide Chrome with a guide to show you where the error really happened. This is extremely helpful for debugging. First, you need to build the source map.

To build the source map, you can use the gulp-sourcemaps plug-in. Because it needs to wrap a few other plug-ins, this one works a bit different from the other Gulp plug-ins:

```
$ npm install --save gulp-sourcemaps
```

Then edit your Gulp task like the following:

```
var gulp = require('gulp')
var concat = require('gulp-concat')
var sourcemaps = require('gulp-sourcemaps')
var uglify = require('gulp-uglify')
var ngAnnotate = require('gulp-ng-annotate')
```

```
gulp.task('js', function () {
  gulp.src(['ng/module.js', 'ng/**/*.js'])
    .pipe(sourcemaps.init())
      .pipe(concat('app.js'))
      .pipe(ngAnnotate())
      .pipe(uglify())
    .pipe(sourcemaps.write())
    .pipe(gulp.dest('assets'))
})

gulp.task('watch:js', ['js'], function () {
  gulp.watch('ng/**/*.js', ['js'])
})
```

If you now look at app.js, you'll see it has a huge comment in there that actually contains the contents of all the preminified files. You will also see the console log now correctly points to posts.svc.js with a friendly callstack. Having confirmed this, you can remove the console.error from posts.svc.js.

You now have a great Gulp task to build all of your JavaScript. As you've seen, Gulp is pretty composable. For example, if you want to add something like CoffeeScript, it would be easy to do.

On some projects, I will have a separate task to generate JavaScript for development versus production. Typically the development one won't do any minification. If there are a lot of assets and minification takes a long time, a setup like that might be preferable. Still, to maintain parity between production and development, I do encourage you to build the JavaScript the same in both environments.

BUILDING CSS WITH GULP

Pretty much all web apps today use some kind of CSS preprocessor (Sass, Less, Stylus, and so on). These have features such as variables (to put color codes in), mixins, includes, and so on.

Sass is probably the most popular CSS preprocessor right now, but it has a couple downsides. First, it's really slow. Large apps can take several minutes to fully compile. It's also written in Ruby, which would require you to install Ruby on your machines and make sure it's configured properly.

Stylus is a newer CSS preprocessor that has some features you won't find in Sass (powerful logic, ability to run Node.js inside, and an optional cleaner syntax. It's also written in Node, so using it is easy. For these reasons, you'll be using Stylus on this project. If you want to use an alternate, though, it's a similar setup.

You won't be working with CSS much in this book, so to get a quick example going, let's just change the <h1> to be green.

My favorite part of Stylus is the flexibility in the syntax. You are free to write the same CSS many different ways. Here's an example of four ways to write the same Stylus.

Normal syntax:

```
h1 {
  color: green;
}
```

Semicolons are optional:

```
h1 {
  color: green
}
```

Curly braces are optional too:

```
h1
  color: green
```

Even the colon is optional:

```
h1
  color green
```

Create a file `css/app.styl` with one of those variations.

Next, install `gulp-stylus`:

```
$ npm install --save gulp-stylus
```

Now you could add a new task to gulpfile.js, but since Gulp files tend to get pretty big, this would be a nice time to split the Gulp config into separate files. Create a file gulp/css.js with the following content:

```
var gulp   = require('gulp')
var stylus = require('gulp-stylus')

gulp.task('css', function () {
  gulp.src('css/**/*.styl')
    .pipe(stylus())
    .pipe(gulp.dest('assets'))
})
```

Then let's put a bit of code into the gulpfile.js file to read in all of the files under /gulp:

```
var fs = require('fs')
fs.readdirSync(__dirname + '/gulp').forEach(function (task) {
  require('./gulp/' + task)
})
```

If this code is confusing, you could just add each Gulp task with individual require()s. I just do this so that I don't have to add a new require() every time I create a new Gulp file.

Now any files you add to /gulp will be automatically included. I suggest breaking out the JavaScript building part of gulpfile.js into a file /gulp/scripts.js.

Run this task:

```
$ gulp css
```

Then include the CSS in /layouts/posts.html, like so:

```
<link rel="stylesheet" href="/app.css">
```

And you should have a green header! Read up on Stylus at *http://learnboost.github.io/stylus* for more on how to use it.

I also suggest a task watch:css like you had for the JavaScript so you don't have to run the task all the time:

```
gulp.task('watch:css', function () {
  gulp.watch('css/**/*.styl', ['css'])
})
```

There is a lot more you could do with the CSS. You could include another source map for the CSS, add tools to help add background-image tags, or run the CSS through a minifier.

GULP DEV TASK

This is great for making sure the CSS keeps getting updated, but it's a bit of a pain since you now have three processes to keep running: the server, gulp watch:js, and gulp watch:css. I like to create a task gulp dev that just runs everything that needs to run while working on the application.

For these kinds of "metatasks," it's best to keep them inside the main gulpfile.js. Add a task in there like the following:

```
gulp.task('dev', ['watch:css', 'watch:js'])
```

Now if you run gulp dev, it'll watch both the CSS and JavaScript files for updates. Note that having a function block for Gulp tasks is optional. This one just depends on two others.

GULP-NODEMON

Now that your assets are being compiled, let's add a Gulp task to start nodemon to run your app for you.

First, install gulp-nodemon:

```
$ npm install --save gulp-nodemon
```

Now create the file /gulp/server.js with the following task:

```
var gulp = require('gulp')
var nodemon = require('gulp-nodemon')

gulp.task('dev:server', function () {
  nodemon({
    script: 'server.js',
    ext:    'js'
  })
})
```

You can now run `gulp dev:server` to boot your app. It'll automatically restart if there are any changes to files ending in `.js`. One annoying thing about it is that it reboots even for non-Node code changes, causing a lot of restarts while working on the app. To exclude non-Node files, add an `ignore` section to the config:

```
gulp.task('dev:server', function () {
  nodemon({
    script: 'server.js',
    ext:    'js',
    ignore: ['ng*', 'gulp*', 'assets*']
  })
})
```

You'll want to keep that `ignore` section updated as you add more and more JavaScript files to your application.

Now that you have the server working with `gulp dev:server`, let's include it in `gulp dev`:

```
gulp.task('dev', ['watch:css', 'watch:js', 'dev:server'])
```

Now `gulp dev` will run all the processes you need to build your application. If there were other tasks you could run, you could just add it to Gulp. Since those Gulp tasks are just Node functions, you could do anything you want in a task. It's usually used for asset compilation, but as you saw with `gulp-nodemon`, that's certainly not the only use case.

OTHER GULP PLUG-INS

Here are some other Gulp plug-ins worth checking out:

- **gulp-jshint**: Runs a linter over your JavaScript to see whether it meets your code standards
- **gulp-rev**: Appends the hash of the contents of a file to the filename, which is really useful for aggressive caching, which you'll use later
- **gulp-autoprefixer**: Adds vendor prefixes to CSS automatically
- **gulp-rimraf**: Cleans out directories to get a fresh build
- **gulp-imagemin**: Compresses images
- **gulp-livereload**: Automatically refreshes the browser when CSS/JavaScript changes

NEXT STEPS

The project now has a fleshed-out and extensible build process driven by Gulp. With this in place, you can start building features in your application.

## CHAPTER 7

Building Authentication in Node.js

In the previous chapter, you automated the building of the application with Gulp. You'll shift gears here and move on to authentication. In this chapter, you will be building a new, demo authentication app in Node.js outside of the social app you've been building. In the next chapter, you will integrate this authentication strategy into your social app.

INTRODUCING TOKEN AUTHENTICATION

In any application, you need to authenticate the user making the requests to the server. There are two ways to do this with an Angular application:

- **Cookie-based authentication**: This works like a traditional web application. You set a session cookie on a login page that will then be used by all later requests. This method requires building forms on the Node side that are traditional HTTP-generated pages.
- **Token-based authentication**: This method works more like an API. It uses a signed token that the client must send on every request. The client can get the token via an API.

For this book, you will be using the token-based approach. The cookie-based approach is a bit easier to set up, but it is inflexible. Using tokens, you can come up with clever ways to authenticate the user and provide a more seamless experience. It also eases debugging and troubleshooting since you just need the token to interact with the API. It also allows the API to be accessed via a mobile app in the same way. It helps with performance since the token is validated using an algorithm rather than a database hit on every request.

The main benefit, though, is that it decouples your client app from your server. This makes it easier to understand the login flow in the system as well since there are fewer moving parts.

This chapter is all about Node and Express instrumented through curl. In the next chapter, you'll integrate this authentication into Angular.

JSON WEB TOKEN (JWT)

JWT (pronounced "jot") is a standard format designed for this specific purpose (authentication). It is simple and could be implemented in any programming language even if a library does not exist.

Functionally, in Node, you can use the npm package `jwt-simple` to create these tokens on the server side. You can create a JWT with the encode function like so:

```
var jwt = require('jwt-simple')
var token = jwt.encode({username: 'dickeyxxx'}, 'supersecretkey')
// token is now: eyJ0eXAiOiJKV1QiLCJhbGciOiJIUzI1NiJ9.
→ eyJ1c2VybmFtZSI6ImRpY2tleXh4eCJ9.0w1RshE-2k7r94VmFZeSH_JBOTAg9OEecznduMwaEGc
```

That token contains the object you passed in as the first argument to encode and signed with the second. It's important to understand that JWT does *not* encrypt that object, but only signs it. I'm going to take the rest of this section to explain how JWT works under the hood. If this is over your head, that's fine; it's only important to understand that JWT signs and not encrypts, not how it works.

All JWTs are split into three parts separated by periods (.).

In this example, the first section, eyJ0eXAiOiJKV1QiLCJhbGciOiJIUzI1NiJ9, is a base64 representation of the header. If you decode it (try using www.jwt.io), you get the following data:

```
{"typ":"JWT","alg":"HS256"}
```

This says that the token is a JWT and that the algorithm HMAC256 was used to sign the token. There are more headers that can be sent to say who signed it, when it was signed, when it should expire, and more.

The second section, eyJ1c2VybmFtZSI6ImRpY2tleXh4eCJ9, is the payload. This is the base64-encoded object you passed in with the first argument. If you run this through the decoder, you get the following:

```
{"username":"dickeyxxx"}
```

Note that you didn't have to use that secret to get this data! This means the client, or anyone with a token, can read what is in it! It's important to know that so you don't store secure data in here, but it could also be useful. The client, in this case, can find out the username of the current user from the token alone without having to make an HTTP call.

Also, if you have a service-oriented architecture, this is how you can validate requests from any server without having to communicate with a central authentication server. Any server with that secret can validate and generate these tokens without communicating with each other.

The last section is the signature. It is not base64 encoded. It tells the server that the payload is valid. If you were to try to change the payload to match a different user, the signature would no longer match, and jwt-simple would immediately reject it. This is where the power of JWT comes into play.

JWT WITH EXPRESS

To use JWT in an application, I will show how to build a small Express server that has two endpoints:

- POST /session: Sending a username/password will return a JWT.
- GET /user: Passing in a JWT token will return the information about the current user.

Note that this is a new, separate app from the social app. In the next chapter you will be integrating this method of authentication into your social app.

I'll build this up in a series of steps to show how each part works. First, let's just get the server sending and receiving JWT tokens. Install jwt-simple:

```
$ npm install --save jwt-simple
```

Then create a file called server.js with this code:

```
var express = require('express')
var jwt = require('jwt-simple')
var app = express()
app.use(require('body-parser').json())

var secretKey  = 'supersecretkey'

app.post('/session', function (req, res) {
  var username = req.body.username
  // TODO: Validate password
  var token = jwt.encode({username: username}, secretKey)
  res.json(token)
})

app.get('/user', function (req, res) {
  var token = req.headers['x-auth']
  var user = jwt.decode(token, secretKey)
  // TODO: pull user info from database
  res.json(user)
})

app.listen(3000)
```

And start it up with this:

```
$ nodemon server-auth.js
```

If you hit the server with a POST /session to get a token, like so:

```
$ curl -X POST -d '{"username": "dickeyxxx"}' -H "Content-Type:
→ application/json" localhost:3000/session
```

you get the following JWT:

```
eyJ0eXAiOiJKV1QiLCJhbGciOiJIUzI1NiJ9.e30.
→ FElHZuJXT8VQAJMx2hjJ17bLXldLKBxuwFXMZJzHAUY
```

Then if you pass that token in the X-Auth header to GET /user:

```
$ curl -H "X-Auth: eyJ0eXAiOiJKV1QiLCJhbGciOiJIUzI1NiJ9.
→ eyJ1c2VybmFtZSI6ImRpY2tleXh4eCJ9.Ow1RshE-2k7r94VmFZeSH_
→ JBOTAg90EecznduMwaEGc" localhost:3000/user
```

you get the token, decrypted, as shown here:

```
{"username":"dickeyxxx"}
```

The server is now generating and decoding tokens for you, but it's not that interesting since it's not actually pulling data from anywhere. To make this work, first I'll show how to use a static user array in memory, and then you'll move it over to MongoDB.

Note that there is a more standard Authorization HTTP header you could use in place of my X-Auth header, but that requires you to pass the type in addition to the token. It would look like this:

```
Authorization: Basic [jwt]
```

It is fine to use but requires a bit of string splitting and concatenation I find burdensome. It's fine to come up with your own header types, but you're supposed to add X- to the front.

PASSWORD VALIDATION

If you had a user array like the following:

```
[{ username: 'dickeyxxx', password: 'pass' }]
```

you could replace your app with the following code (npm install --save lodash first):

```
var express = require('express')
var jwt = require('jwt-simple')
var _ = require('lodash')
var app = express()
app.use(require('body-parser').json())
```

```
var users = [{username: 'dickeyxxx', password: 'pass'}]
var secretKey = 'supersecretkey'

function findUserByUsername(username) {
  return _.find(users, {username: username})
}

function validateUser(user, password) {
  return user.password === password
}

app.post('/session', function (req, res) {
  var user = findUserByUsername(req.body.username)
  if (!validateUser(user, req.body.password)) {
    return res.send(401) // Unauthorized
  }
  var token = jwt.encode({username: user.username}, secretKey)
  res.json(token)
})

app.get('/user', function (req, res) {
  var token = req.headers['x-auth']
  var user = jwt.decode(token, secretKey)
  // TODO: pull user info from database
  res.json(user)
})

app.listen(3000)

$ curl -X POST -d '{"username": "dickeyxxx", "password":"pass"}' -H
 → "Content-Type: application/json" localhost:3000/session

"eyJ0eXAiOiJKV1QiLCJhbGciOiJIUzI1NiJ9.eyJ1c2VybmFtZSI6ImRpY2tleXh4eCJ9.
 → Ow1RshE-2k7r94VmFZeSH_JBOTAg9OEecznduMwaEGc"
```

I added a couple of helper functions, findUserByUsername and validateUser, that will look up the user in the "database" and check their password, respectively. I'm using Lo-Dash's find function to quickly do the lookup logic rather than looping over the users array until I find one. (Lo-Dash is a utility library to help perform common JavaScript tasks; see *http://lodash.com/*.)

The major issue with this code is that you're putting the plain-text password into the "database." (Later it'll be MongoDB instead of this static array, but it's important to work through this iteratively since authentication has a lot going on.)

USING BCRYPT

You know it's insecure to store plain-text passwords in the database. That would make it easy for someone to find the passwords for all users. One improvement you can make over plain text is to use encryption. Encryption is still a bad way to store passwords, though, since having the key would allow you to simply decrypt the passwords. Therefore, encryption is a totally insecure way to store passwords.

The secure way to deal with passwords is by using a hashing algorithm. A *hash* is a one-way algorithm. You store the hash result in the database, and then when checking a password, you hash it and compare the result with the hash stored in the database. There is no way to go from the hash back to the original password. Also, having the hash isn't enough to get a password that matches it (at least without a rainbow table). So if somehow a hacker got a hash for a user's password, they still couldn't actually log in.

I won't get into the specifics of the algorithm, but research the terms *rainbow tables* and *password salting* to learn more.

There are still problems with straight hashing like rainbow tables or brute-force attacks. The best solution today for dealing with passwords is BCrypt. BCrypt is a hashing algorithm that is intentionally slow, making brute-force attacks too expensive to do.

Like JWT, it's not really important to understand how it works, just how to use it. To find the bcrypt hash of your *pass* password, you can calculate it inside a Node console:

```
$ npm install --save bcrypt
$ node
> require('bcrypt').hashSync('pass', 10)
'$2a$10$Jmo/n32ofSM9JvzfHOz6Me6TMyn6C/U9JhzDG8xhQC4ExHMG1jXz2'
```

The 10 is the number of rounds you want it to pass over to generate the hash. More rounds is more secure but slower (10 is sufficient for almost anything).

Note that running it again results in a different hash. This is because it's salted randomly. You can validate the password with compareSync:

```
> require('bcrypt').compareSync('pass', '$2a$10$Jmo/n32ofSM9JvzfHOz6Me6TMyn6C/
→ U9JhzDG8xhQC4ExHMG1jXz2')
true
```

You could now put that password hash into the users array and edit your validateUser function to use it:

```
var bcrypt = require('bcrypt')
function validateUser(user, password) {
  return bcrypt.compareSync(password, user.password)
}
```

This would work, but it's synchronous (the enemy of JavaScript development). In other words, while validating the password, everything else is blocked, and you want to avoid that. In my tests, the asynchronous version could handle about four times as many requests, each one about three times faster. You can move this to the asynchronous version by using a callback (as we discussed in Chapter 2), but you'll have to call your validateUser function with a callback as well.

The final version of the BCrypt version of this code is shown here:

```
var express = require('express')
var jwt = require('jwt-simple')
var _ = require('lodash')
var app = express()
var bcrypt = require('bcrypt')
app.use(require('body-parser').json())

var users = [{username: 'dickeyxxx', password: '$2a$10$Jmo/
  n32ofSM9JvzfHOz6Me6TMyn6C/U9JhzDG8xhQC4ExHMG1jXz2'}]
var secretKey = 'supersecretkey'

function findUserByUsername(username) {
  return _.find(users, {username: username})
}

function validateUser(user, password, cb) {
  bcrypt.compare(password, user.password, cb)
}

app.post('/session', function (req, res) {
  var user = findUserByUsername(req.body.username)
  validateUser(user, req.body.password, function (err, valid) {
    if (err || !valid) { return res.send(401) }
    var token = jwt.encode({username: user.username}, secretKey)
    res.json(token)
  })
})

app.get('/user', function (req, res) {
  var token = req.headers['x-auth']
```

```
  var user = jwt.decode(token, secretKey)
  // TODO: pull user info from database
  res.json(user)
})

app.listen(3000)
```

AUTHENTICATION WITH MongoDB

Now let's finish the demo authentication app by adding a real database into the mix. First, create a user model with Mongoose in a new file called user.js, like so:

```
var mongoose = require('mongoose')
mongoose.connect('mongodb://localhost/auth_demo')

var user = mongoose.Schema({
  username: String,
  password: String
})

module.exports = mongoose.model('User', user)
```

Then, add this line to the top of server-auth.js:

```
var User = require('./user')
```

Now in the same file, let's create a route POST /user to create new user accounts:

```
app.post('/user', function (req, res, next) {
  var user = new User({username: req.body.username})
  bcrypt.hash(req.body.password, 10, function (err, hash) {
    user.password = hash
    user.save(function (err, user) {
      if (err) { throw next(err) }
      res.send(201)
    })
  })
})
```

Now you are creating users with a bcrypt-generated hash. To create a user with curl, use this:

```
$ curl -X POST -d '{"username": "dickeyxxx", "password": "pass"}' -H
→ "Content-Type: application/json" localhost:3000/user
```

Then if you update your POST /session route to look into Mongo for a corresponding user, you get this:

```
app.post('/session', function (req, res, next) {
  User.findOne({username: req.body.username}, function (err, user) {
    if (err) { return next(err) }
    if (!user) { return res.send(401) }
    bcrypt.compare(req.body.password, user.password, function (err, valid) {
      if (err) { return next(err) }
      if (!valid) { return res.send(401) }
      var token = jwt.encode({username: user.username}, secretKey)
      res.json(token)
    })
  })
})
```

First it looks up a user matching the username using Mongoose's findOne() method. If it finds one, it checks the password against the one sent in. If everything is successful, it builds a JWT and sends it back, sending a 401 header or error response otherwise. You can use curl in the same way you did earlier now.

Updating the GET /user endpoint to do a database lookup as well is easy now:

```
app.get('/user', function (req, res) {
  var token = req.headers['x-auth']
  var auth = jwt.decode(token, secretKey)
  User.findOne({username: auth.username}, function (err, user) {
    res.json(user)
  })
})
```

It might look a little strange that I'm taking in the base64-encoded username (that the client can easily see) and directly pulling the user who matches it out of the database. Remember, though, it's securely signed; if the user changed it, the signature wouldn't match, and it would be invalid.

The way this code works right now is that it will send back the full user object with the password hash. Even though bcrypt is pretty safe, it's probably not a good idea to send this down to the client. You can prevent this from happening by setting select: false in the model:

```
var mongoose = require('mongoose')
mongoose.connect('mongodb://localhost/auth_demo')

var user = mongoose.Schema({
  username: String,
  password: {type: String, select: false}
})

module.exports = mongoose.model('User', user)
```

But you'll need to explicitly ask for this in POST /session since you actually do need to pull the password hash in that case.

With that final change, here is the final code for this authentication demo:

```
var express = require('express')
var jwt = require('jwt-simple')
var app = express()
var bcrypt = require('bcrypt')
var User = require('./user')
app.use(require('body-parser').json())

var secretKey  = 'supersecretkey'

app.post('/session', function (req, res, next) {
  User.findOne({username: req.body.username})
  .select('password')
  .exec(function (err, user) {
    if (err) { return next(err) }
    if (!user) { return res.send(401) }
    bcrypt.compare(req.body.password, user.password, function (err, valid) {
      if (err) { return next(err) }
      if (!valid) { return res.send(401) }
      var token = jwt.encode({username: user.username}, secretKey)
      res.json(token)
```

```
    })
  })
})

app.get('/user', function (req, res) {
  var token = req.headers['x-auth']
  var auth = jwt.decode(token, secretKey)
  User.findOne({username: auth.username}, function (err, user) {
    res.json(user)
  })
})

app.post('/user', function (req, res, next) {
  var user = new User({username: req.body.username})
  bcrypt.hash(req.body.password, 10, function (err, hash) {
    user.password = hash
    user.save(function (err) {
      if (err) { throw next(err) }
      res.send(201)
    })
  })
})

app.listen(3000)
```

NEXT STEPS

In order for you to integrate this into your social application, you'll also need a client-side router. In the next chapter, you'll learn how the router works and integrate your authentication strategy into it.

CHAPTER 8

Adding Routing and Client Authentication

In the previous chapter, you saw how to build up an authentication API with Node and Express. Now, you will take that code and integrate it into your application. The goal is that when you are complete, only users will be able to make posts, and the posts will be linked to the currently logged-in user.

ROUTING

Before you can build up the pages for authentication, you'll need to include Angular's router. Angular has a module you can add to your app and turn it into a single-page application. Angular will be able to show different views based on the URL.

Before you get started with that, let's rename the layout file `layouts/posts.html` to `layouts/app.html`. This is because your layout file will now be used across all pages, not just the posts view. Make sure you update `controllers/static.js` to point to `layouts/app.html` as well.

The router (`ng-route`) does not come included in the main Angular code, so you need to include it and declare it as a dependency in your app.

Go into `layouts/app.html` and add `ng-route` after the Angular script tag. The bottom of `layouts/app.html` should look like this:

```
<script src='https://ajax.googleapis.com/ajax/libs/angularjs/1.2.18/
→ angular.js'></script>
<script src='https://ajax.googleapis.com/ajax/libs/angularjs/1.2.18/
→ angular-route.js'></script>
<script src='/app.js'></script>
</body>
</html>
```

After adding the new `<script>` tag, go into `ng/module.js` and declare `ng-route` as a dependency:

```
angular.module('app', [
  'ngRoute'
])
```

It might look a little strange that I added newlines for this. This is because there will likely be many modules you want to declare as dependencies. Having each one on a newline will look much better in source control since you will easily be able to see what module was added with what commit. It's also easier to manage as it grows.

Now add a new file `ng/routes.js` to define your routes for the posts page, register page, and login page. Soon, you'll add functionality behind these, but it won't break anything having routes that point nowhere.

```
angular.module('app')
.config(function ($routeProvider) {
  $routeProvider
  .when('/', { controller: 'PostsCtrl', templateUrl: 'posts.html' })
```

```
.when('/register', { controller: 'RegisterCtrl', templateUrl:
⇒ 'register.html' })
.when('/login', { controller: 'LoginCtrl', templateUrl: 'login.html' })
})
```

Each route has a `controller` and `templateUrl` associated with it. When you add the `ng-view` directive to `layouts/app.html`, it will be swapped out with the controller and template matching the route. Add this directive to `layouts/app.html` now right after the opening `<body>` tag:

```
<div ng-view></div>
```

Now if you start your app with this:

```
$ gulp dev
```

and load *localhost:3000* in a browser, you'll see a 404 error in the JavaScript console because it is trying to load the `posts.html` template file. The router loads these templates on demand. You'll need to create a new file called `posts.html` that Express can serve to your application.

Create a file called `templates/posts.html` with the following content from `layouts/app.html`. You do not need to specify `ng-controller` since it is now in the routing config:

```
<div class='container'>
  <h1>Recent Posts</h1>
  <form role='form'>
    <div class='form-group'>
      <div class='input-group'>
        <input ng-model='postBody' class='form-control' />
        <span class='input-group-btn'>
          <button ng-click='addPost()' class='btn btn-default'>
          ⇒ Add Post</button>
        </span>
      </div>
    </div>
  </form>
  <ul class='list-group'>
    <li ng-repeat="post in posts | orderBy:'-date'" class='list-group-item'>
      <strong>@{{ post.username }}</strong>
      <span>{{ post.body }}</span>
    </li>
  </ul>
</div>
```

Now remove that HTML from `layouts/app.html` since it will be loaded from here. Your `layouts/app.html` should be simple now:

```
<!DOCTYPE html>
<html>
<head>
  <link rel="stylesheet" href="http://netdna.bootstrapcdn.com/bootstrap/3.1.1/
  → css/bootstrap.min.css">
  <link rel="stylesheet" href="/app.css">
</head>
<body ng-app='app'>
  <div ng-view></div>
  <script src='https://ajax.googleapis.com/ajax/libs/angularjs/1.2.18/
  → angular.js'></script>
  <script src='https://ajax.googleapis.com/ajax/libs/angularjs/1.2.18/
  → angular-route.js'></script>
  <script src='/app.js'></script>
</body>
</html>
```

Next let's get Express to serve the `templates` folder. Open `controllers/static.js` and add the following line:

```
router.use(express.static(__dirname + '/../templates'))
```

Your app should now be back to where it was before. The difference is that the main layout file is simple. It just declares an `ng-view` directive. `ng-route` is asynchronously loading `templates/posts.html` to render the page. It knows to pick that template and controller based on the config code in `ng/routes.js`.

CREATING A LOGIN FORM

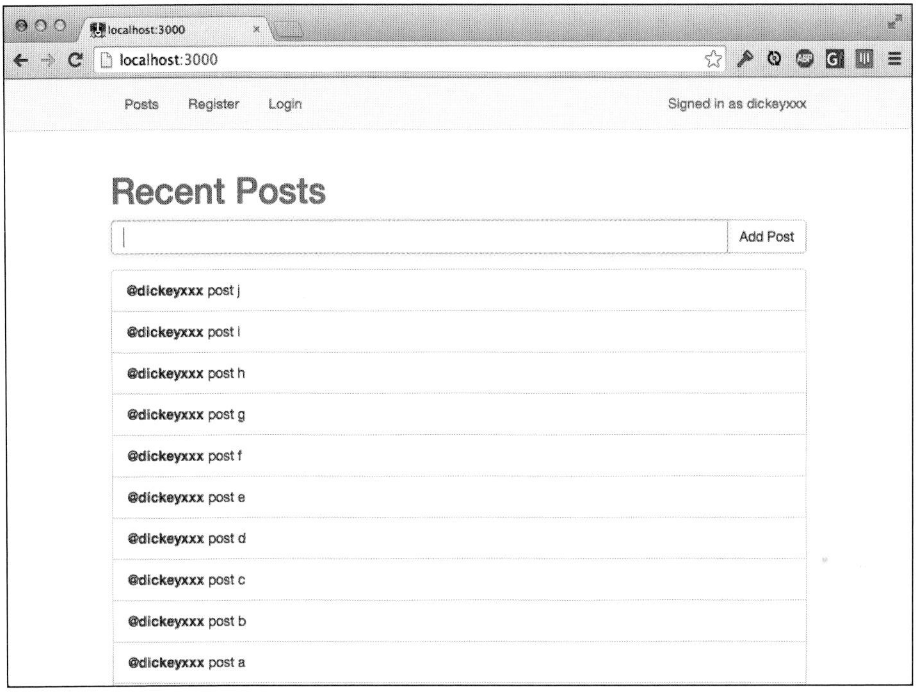

FIGURE 8.1 Navbar example

Now that you have your router set up, let's add a login page to your app. It will look like **Figure 8.1**.

First, let's get links to the posts, login, and register pages inside `layouts/app.html`. Before `ng-view`, add the following header with Bootstrap styling:

```
<nav class='navbar navbar-default'>
  <div class='container'>
    <ul class='nav navbar-nav'>
      <li><a href="/#/">Posts</a></li>
      <li><a href="/#/register">Register</a></li>
      <li><a href="/#/login">Login</a></li>
    </ul>
  </div>
</nav>
```

Note these routes use the hash prefix method of routing. Later, you'll see how to move this to using HTML5 pushstate, allowing you to remove the hash from the URLs. It's not as pretty, but the hash method is easier to set up and debug.

Now clicking the Login button in the bar will update your URL to *http://localhost:3000/#/login*. Clicking it will trigger a load to `templates/login.html`, which doesn't exist. Let's create that now:

```html
<div class="container">
  <form ng-submit="login(username, password)">
    <div class="form-group">
      <label>Username</label>
      <input class="form-control" type="text" ng-model="username">
    </div>
    <div class="form-group">
      <label>Password</label>
      <input class="form-control" type="password" ng-model="password">
    </div>
    <input class="btn btn-success btn-lg btn-block" type="submit"
    → value="Login">
  </form>
</div>
```

This is a basic Angular login form that will be looking for a `login()` function on the `$scope` object of its controller. The matching controller looks like this and goes in `ng/login.ctrl.js`:

```javascript
angular.module('app')
.controller('LoginCtrl', function ($scope, UserSvc) {
  $scope.login = function (username, password) {
    UserSvc.login(username, password)
    .then(function (user) {
      console.log(user)
    })
  }
})
```

What you're doing here is calling the `.login()` function on a user service (yet to be created), and on success, you just log out the current user to see whether login is working. There just isn't a lot you're able to do with the user just yet.

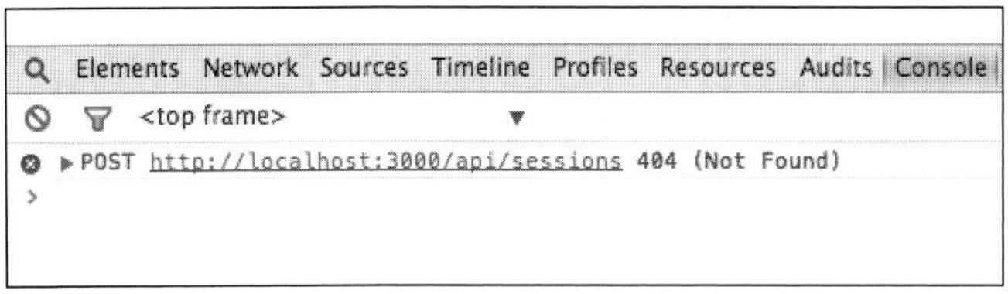

FIGURE 8.2 404 error loading *http://localhost:3000/api/sessions*

Here is the code for your UserSvc that goes in ng/user.svc.js:

```javascript
angular.module('app')
.service('UserSvc', function ($http) {
  var svc = this
  svc.getUser = function () {
    return $http.get('/api/users', {
      headers: { 'X-Auth': this.token }
    })
  }
  svc.login = function (username, password) {
    return $http.post('/api/sessions', {
      username: username, password: password
    }).then(function (val) {
      svc.token = val.data
      return svc.getUser()
    })
  }
})
```

The login process has two steps. First, you call POST /api/sessions to get a JWT; then, you call GET /api/users to get the currently logged-in user's information. You could have the server send that data back right in the login callback, but it's good to keep your API requests as simple as possible to promote reuse. Also, Node and Angular are so fast that this will all happen quickly.

Attempting to fill out the form will now give you a 404 because you haven't built that part of the app (see **Figure 8.2**).

It's a good idea, however, to check to see whether the username and password are being passed in the Network tab in Chrome (or whatever dev tools in the browser you're using provides).

EXPRESS AUTHENTICATION

Now that you have Angular requesting a JWT through POST /api/sessions, let's port over some of the code from the previous chapter to serve JWTs through your app.

First, create the user model based on the previous chapter's code in models/user.js:

```
var db = require('../db')
var user = db.Schema({
  username: { type: String, required: true },
  password: { type: String, required: true, select: false}
})
module.exports = db.model('User', user)
```

Remember, you set select: false on the password field, so you don't send it down to the client.

Next, you'll need to store the private key for creating the JWTs in a place that can be accessed by many parts of the Express app. This is a good time to add a config file for your application.

Create a file config.js in the root of the project:

```
module.exports = {
  secret: 'supersecretkey'
}
```

This is a good place to put API keys, database configuration, or settings that can change from development to production. You won't be doing this now, but the convention is to set the NODE_ENV environment variable to production when in production and check for that inside this config.js file.

Now mount the new controllers inside server.js:

```
app.use('/api/sessions', require('./controllers/api/sessions'))
app.use('/api/users', require('./controllers/api/users'))
```

And create the sessions controller at controllers/api/sessions.js:

```
var router = require('express').Router()
var User = require('../../models/user')
var bcrypt = require('bcrypt')
var jwt = require('jwt-simple')
var config = require('../../config')
```

```
router.post('/', function (req, res, next) {
  User.findOne({username: req.body.username})
  .select('password').select('username')
  .exec(function (err, user) {
    if (err) { return next(err) }
    if (!user) { return res.send(401) }
    bcrypt.compare(req.body.password, user.password, function (err, valid) {
      if (err) { return next(err) }
      if (!valid) { return res.send(401) }
      var token = jwt.encode({username: user.username}, config.secret)
      res.send(token)
    })
  })
})

module.exports = router
```

Make sure you also use `npm install bcrypt` and `jwt-simple` to install those tools into your project.

This is largely the same code you built in the demo app. It looks up a user from the passed-in username and then checks the password hash with bcrypt against the one the user sent in. If successful, it will pass back a new JWT for that user.

That JWT is what the client will need to make all future authenticated requests.

Now that you have your sessions controller, create the users controller at controllers/api/users.js:

```
var router = require('express').Router()
var bcrypt = require('bcrypt')
var jwt = require('jwt-simple')
var User = require('../../models/user')
var config = require('../../config')

router.get('/', function (req, res, next) {
  if (!req.headers['x-auth']) {
    return res.send(401)
  }
  var auth = jwt.decode(req.headers['x-auth'], config.secret)
  User.findOne({username: auth.username}, function (err, user) {
    if (err) { return next(err) }
```

```
    res.json(user)
  })
})

router.post('/', function (req, res, next) {
  var user = new User({username: req.body.username})
  bcrypt.hash(req.body.password, 10, function (err, hash) {
    if (err) { return next(err) }
    user.password = hash
    user.save(function (err) {
      if (err) { return next(err) }
      res.send(201)
    })
  })
})

module.exports = router
```

This controller has two actions: one to get an existing user and the other to create a new user.

You're almost done with authentication. Create a new user with curl so that you can test it with your Angular app's login functionality:

```
$ curl -X POST -d '{"username": "dickeyxxx", "password": "pass"}' -H
→ "Content-Type: application/json" localhost:3000/api/users
```

Now you should be able to log in with this user. Remember, all logging in does right now is print out to the console (see **Figure 8.3**).

You can also try logging in as anyone else to trigger the 401 Unauthorized response. If you see output like that, you're good to go.

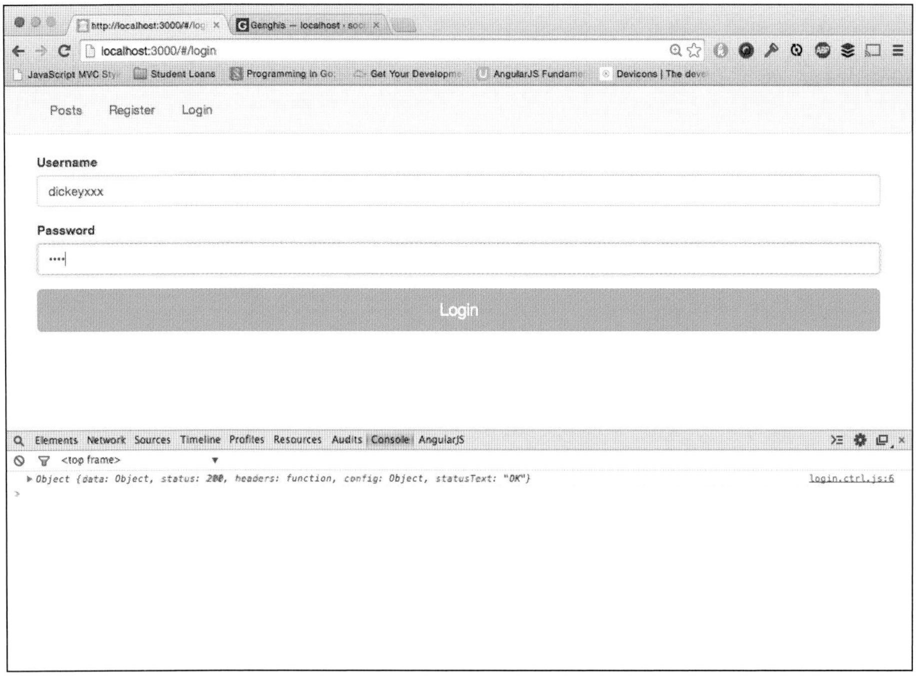

FIGURE 8.3 User info logging out to console after creating a session

ANGULAR EVENTS

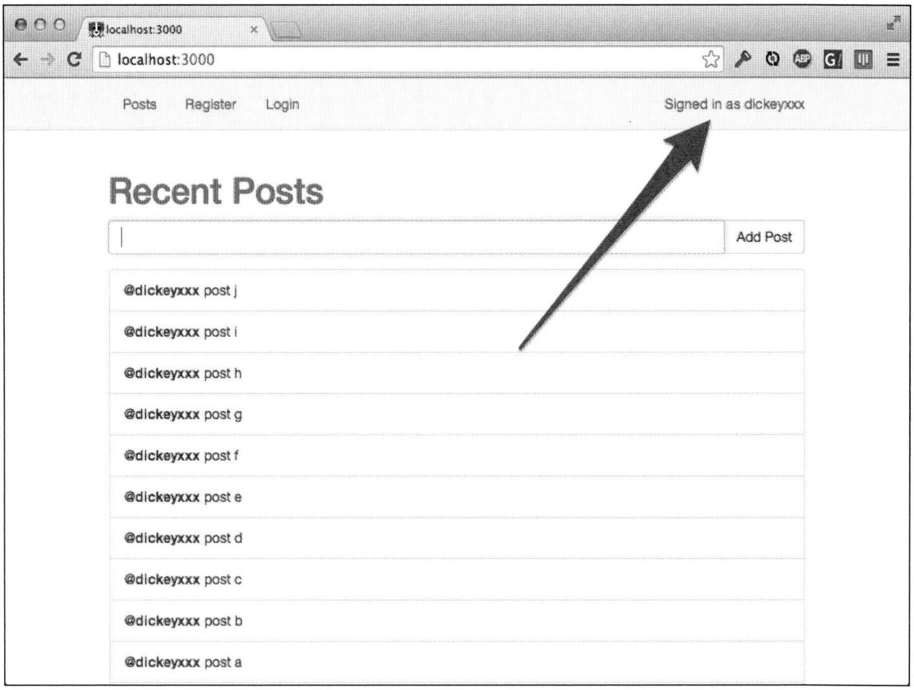

FIGURE 8.4 Currently logged-in user

What you want to do is show the currently logged-in user in the upper-right corner of the screen, on the nav bar. It will look like **Figure 8.4**.

Go ahead and add update your nav bar in layouts/app.html:

```
<nav class='navbar navbar-default'>
  <div class='container'>
    <ul class='nav navbar-nav'>
      <li><a href="/#/">Posts</a></li>
      <li><a href="/#/register">Register</a></li>
      <li><a href="/#/login">Login</a></li>
    </ul>
    <p ng-if='currentUser' class="navbar-text navbar-right">
      Signed in as {{currentUser.username}}
    </p>
  </div>
</nav>
```

Now you can populate that `currentUser` object on $scope here. It isn't as easy as going into `LoginCtrl` and setting `$scope.currentUser = user`, however. That's because `LoginCtrl` isn't scoped all the way out to this controller. You could use `$rootScope` (the global scope) instead, but there is a better way to do this without messing with global memory like that.

The better solution is to have the `LoginCtrl` bubble up a login event and have a parent `ApplicationCtrl` listen for that. `ApplicationCtrl` will then set `$scope.currentUser`, making it available to all children.

Update `LoginCtrl` in `ng/login.ctrl.js` to pass the event up using `$emit`:

```
angular.module('app')
.controller('LoginCtrl', function ($scope, UserSvc) {
  $scope.login = function (username, password) {
    UserSvc.login(username, password)
    .then(function (response) {
      $scope.$emit('login', response.data)
    })
  }
})
```

Now, put the `ng-controller` directive for the `ApplicationCtrl` on the `<body>` tag inside `layouts/app.html`:

```
<body ng-app='app' ng-controller='ApplicationCtrl'>
```

And create `ng/application.ctrl.js`:

```
angular.module('app')
.controller('ApplicationCtrl', function ($scope) {
  $scope.$on('login', function (_, user) {
    $scope.currentUser = user
  })
})
```

Now you should finally be able to log in to your app! One more thing you need to do in order to finish up your authentication is to link the user to the post.

AUTHENTICATING SOCIAL POSTS

Right now, the client is actually sending the username of the posts. What should happen is that the server should find out who the user is based on the JWT. This prevents users from modifying their usernames.

You need to reuse the code in controllers/api/users.js to grab the user's information from the JWT. This is a good time to introduce some custom middleware in your Express app.

Create the file auth.js in the root of the project:

```
var jwt = require('jwt-simple')
var config = require('./config')

module.exports = function (req, res, next) {
  if (req.headers['x-auth']) {
    req.auth = jwt.decode(req.headers['x-auth'], config.secret)
  }
  next()
}
```

This middleware will attach an auth object to the requests for you to look up the current user's information.

Now use this middleware in server.js just before using all the controllers:

```
app.use(require('./auth'))
```

You can now use this code inside controllers/api/posts.js to find the current user's username:

```
router.post('/', function (req, res, next) {
  var post = new Post({body: req.body.body})
  post.username = req.auth.username
  post.save(function (err, post) {
    if (err) { return next(err) }
    res.json(201, post)
  })
})
```

Now the change you need to make in the Angular app is simple; you just need to send up the X-Auth header on the post creation request. You could add this directly to the posts controller, but the better way would be to globally add that header for all requests so you won't have to keep remembering to do that. Update ng/user.svc.js to the following code:

```
angular.module('app')
.service('UserSvc', function ($http) {
  var svc = this
  svc.getUser = function () {
    return $http.get('/api/users')
  }
  svc.login = function (username, password) {
    return $http.post('/api/sessions', {
      username: username, password: password
    }).then(function (val) {
      svc.token = val.data
      $http.defaults.headers.common['X-Auth'] = val.data
      return svc.getUser()
    })
  }
})
```

Now all requests (not just those in this service) will have that header attached. Your app should now be able to make posts based on the current user!

This is a basic demonstration of authentication in Angular. It's definitely not as easy as it is with a traditional web application generated by the server, but it's very flexible. It's also easier to maintain since each component is actually doing very little.

Still, there is more that you could do to turn this into a full-fledged authentication system. I'll briefly describe some tips in the following sections.

HTML5 PUSHSTATE

Enabling pushstate in Angular is easy; all you need to do is dependency inject `$locationProvider` and add this line to your ng/routes.js file:

`$locationProvider.html5Mode(true)`

This is all that needs to happen on the client; you can now remove the #s from the URLs. Still, if you click Refresh while on a different page, you'll get a 404 since Express doesn't know to serve an Angular app for any request. You can fix this by changing the URL for Express from / to *.

I don't suggest doing this if you are just getting started, though. What often happens is Angular will try to load things like template files that may not exist. When that happens, it loads the app again, which in turn tries to load the template file again. This results in a loop that won't end and often crashes the browser window.

It's a problem in development mode only when you haven't created files, but it does make debugging and development harder.

REGISTRATION

In the book, I haven't covered registration. It is easy, though; all you need to do is add a createUser function to your user service that then calls login after it creates the user and then the form/controller to go with it. It's a good exercise that you should try on your own. It demonstrates the reusability of your API.

LOGOUT

The logout functionality is pretty easy; you'll just need to call a function on `ApplicationCtrl` that deletes `currentUser` from its scope. You'll also probably want to call something on the `UserSvc` that will remove the JWT from the requests.

REMEMBER ME

The best way to remember the last user on the page is by using HTML5 pushstate. You could use this simply by swapping out references to `svc.token` inside `UserSvc` and adding in `window.localStorage.token`.

You will also need to check to see whether that token exists when the app is started. If it does, you'll want to have the `ApplicationCtrl` grab the current logged-in user from `UserSvc.getUser()`.

USER FOREIGN KEY

You may have noticed that you are using the user's username as a `string` on the MongoDB model. It would be a good idea to instead store the user's `ObjectId` on the `Post` object. This way, the username can change, and users will keep all of their posts.

If you implement this, look into Mongoose's population feature as a way to pull down the username when `GET /api/posts` is hit.

NEXT STEPS

You have now seen how to integrate authentication into your application. In the next chapter, you will make the application more immersive by streaming in content with WebSockets.

CHAPTER 9

Pushing Notifications with WebSockets

In this chapter, you'll learn how to make applications more interactive by adding WebSockets. WebSockets allow you to push live changes from a server into a browser.

INTRODUCING WEBSOCKETS

In the interest of finding ways to develop more interactive, more immersive applications, browsers now support a new protocol in addition to HTTP: WebSockets. HTTP was pretty much the only way for developers to communicate with browsers for a long time. It's a reliable, relatively quick protocol that developers got by with.

The major downside to HTTP is that it's one-way for web applications. The browser cannot be an HTTP server, which means that the client must initiate any communication. This works well for what the Web was originally designed for (reading documents and viewing media), but it doesn't support heavy interactivity.

As I covered in Chapter 1, Ajax was a groundbreaking technology that helped developers to quickly load new content on pages. Ajax still uses HTTP, though, so anything a server might want to notify a client about (download process, notification, and new content), it has to query for.

To solve this problem, we've come up with various solutions like Flash, Comet, and short- and long-polling. For the most part, these were all complicated hacks needed to get around the problem of a server not being able to ping a client. Luckily, W3C has now standardized WebSockets as a solution. It has good browser support, working on all major mobile devices, Chrome, Firefox, and Safari. It's supported by IE10 and newer. (Note that if you need to support IE9 or older, the tool `socket.io` will help.)

W3C took time to get this API right, and using it in the browser is easy. For this part of the book, you will be working with WebSockets almost entirely from scratch. There are tools out there to abstract some of the complexity away (such as the aforementioned `socket.io`), but they're really only a light layer of abstraction.

HOW WEBSOCKETS WORK

WebSockets works similarly to the low-level TCP layer. It provides a full-duplex channel between your server and the client. It allows either the client or the server to pass messages as strings to one another, unlike TCP, which only sends bytes back and forth.

On a WebSocket-enabled site, a bit of the JavaScript will be run to tell the browser to make a WebSocket connection. Once it's made, it provides an event callback for messages. It's really easy to make a connection from a browser:

```
var connection = new WebSocket('ws://mysite.com')
connection.onmessage = function (e) {
  console.log('message received: ', e.data)
}
```

Again, no libraries are used here. Simply make a new WebSocket object and attach a function to its onmessage event. After it connects, any messages sent from the server will be delivered to this callback.

Typically that e.data attribute will contain a bit of JSON we will parse, but it could be any string or binary blob.

Sending events is easy as well:

```
var connection = new WebSocket('ws://mysite.com')
connection.onmessage = function (e) {
  console.log('message received: ', e.data)
  connection.send('got your message: ' + e.data)
}
```

You can send messages at any time, not just after receiving one. Because the connection is created asynchronously, you can't just call connection.send() directly after creating the connection object, however. If you wanted to send a message right after connecting, you could use the onopen event:

```
var connection = new WebSocket('ws://mysite.com')
connection.onopen = function () {
  connection.send('hello!')
}
```

Unlike HTTP, the server side of this code looks similar; however, you need to use a package for it since it is not built into Node.js.

Using this technology, you can cause the browser to react to changes from any other system easily. For the social application you've been building, you'll add functionality so that if any user posts an update, all other users will see the update pop up live.

WHAT SHOULD YOU USE WEBSOCKETS FOR?

WebSockets can be used for any kind of client-server communication. There isn't really an overhead to using it instead of HTTP. You could remove HTTP from your social application and do all of the data loading and posting via WebSockets, including authentication.

It can have real benefits when it comes to loading data. The client could request small deltas of the data and sync it rather than relying on HTTP to deliver all the content every time it's loaded. An architecture like this would work extremely well in an offline context. When it came online, it could just sync all new data from both sides.

A setup like this might be good for mobile apps, apps that have very live and interactive content (like games), or anywhere else there would be a lot of thrashing of duplicate data via HTTP.

The trouble with WebSockets is that it maintains a persisting connection resulting in a stateful design. State makes distributed computing difficult and forces you to deal with problems such as connection loss. It also adds a significant amount of entropy to a system—in other words, many different states means many different ways bugs can crop up. Therefore, a WebSocket-based platform can be tougher to develop on than a traditional, stateless HTTP-based platform.

For this reason, unless you're building something like a game, I suggest you use WebSockets only for notifications from the server to the client. It's still useful to deliver new content, notifications, or progress updates, but using HTTP for everything else saves you from the complexity that comes from a stateful architecture.

Find the balance that works for you, though.

WEBSOCKETS IN YOUR SOCIAL APP

You can benefit from WebSockets in your social application. It would be great if a user publishing a post from one browser updated all the other browsers currently looking at the site.

Like most elements of coding in the MEAN stack, it's a good idea to build bits up one at a time, testing them with basic tools. Here you'll use a tool called wscat to connect straight to the Node.js WebSockets. Once you have it displaying new posts, you'll integrate Angular to the WebSockets.

Node doesn't come with built-in support for WebSockets, but there are a few packages out there to help with it. My personal favorite is ws. It is very basic and works just like the client code. It attaches to any Node server object, including one that is given to you by Express.

CONNECTING TO A WS WEBSOCKET

To connect to a ws websocket, first install ws into the social app:

```
$ npm install --save ws
```

Also, install ws globally (this will give you access to the debugging tool wscat):

```
$ npm install --global ws
```

Now create a file websockets.js. You will use this from server.js when loading the app.

```
var ws = require('ws')
exports.connect = function (server) {
  var wss = new ws.Server({server: server})
  wss.on('connection', function (ws) {
    ws.send('hello!')
  })
}
```

This defines a function connect that adds WebSockets to a Node server. When a client connects to a WebSocket, the connection event will be called. You then send a message directly to that new client to say "hello!"

Before you can use this, you need to reference it in server.js. Edit the app.listen section to look like the following:

```
# ...
var server = app.listen(3000, function () {
  console.log('Server listening on', 3000)
})
require('./websockets').connect(server)
```

If you'd like, you can put the require up at the top of the file into a websockets variable and reference it down here. I only put the require here for conciseness in the book.

That server object is actually from the Node core (http.Server). Express's app.listen returns it, so the integration with ws is very easy.

Now try to connect to your application. First boot the server and then run the following wscat command:

```
$ wscat -c ws://localhost:3000
connected (press CTRL+C to quit)
< hello!
```

wscat is a tool that can be either a WebSockets server or client. The -c option has it interact as a client. You immediately get the "hello!" response from the server on connecting.

Try experimenting with this a bit before moving on. See whether you can get ws to echo back commands wscat sends.

Now that you have WebSockets connected, let's see whether you can get it to publish new posts.

PUBLISHING NEW POST NOTIFICATIONS

For this section, you'll still be working with Node but having it post to wscat notifications on new posts. You may have noticed the only way to send notifications from the server is by referencing the object you get in the connection callback. You need to be able to do a "broadcast" and deliver a message to all clients at the same time.

First, let's track all the clients in an array inside websockets.js:

```
var _ = require('lodash')
var ws = require('ws')
var clients = []

exports.connect = function (server) {
  var wss = new ws.Server({server: server})
  wss.on('connection', function (ws) {
    clients.push(ws)

    ws.on('close', function () {
      _.remove(clients, ws)
    })
  })
}
```

On connection, you push the new client onto our array. When that client disconnects, you remove it from the list using Lo-Dash. Removing is important since you would get nasty errors attempting to send messages to disconnected clients. Feel free to add `console.log()` statements inside this code to get an idea what is going on.

Now that you have a list of clients to send a broadcast message to, let's add a broadcast function to `websockets.js`:

```
exports.broadcast = function (topic, data) {
  var json = JSON.stringify({topic: topic, data: data})
  clients.forEach(function (client) {
    client.send(json)
  })
}
```

Here you've defined a function broadcast that takes two arguments: a topic (string) and data (the payload, can be any type). The topic is needed to differentiate a message corresponding to a new post or any other reason the client is receiving a message. You simply generate JSON with these arguments, loop through every client, and send them a message with the JSON.

Before moving on, let's see whether it is working by broadcasting new client connections. Add the following code inside the connect function of `websockets.js`:

```
wss.on('connection', function (ws) {
  clients.push(ws)
  exports.broadcast('new client joined')
  # ...
```

Try adding two or three `wscat` connections in different terminal windows to see whether the event is broadcasting correctly.

To broadcast a message on new posts, simply require this `websockets.js` module in the posts controller (`posts.js`) and call its broadcast function after Mongo saves correctly. Pass the post object down as well so the client will be able to render it.

```
var websockets = require('../../websockets')
# ...
router.post('/', function (req, res, next) {
  var post = new Post({body: req.body.body})
  post.username = req.auth.username
  post.save(function (err, post) {
    if (err) { return next(err) }
    websockets.broadcast('new_post', post)
    res.json(201, post)
  })
})
```

Now try creating a post in the browser while you have a wscat session open. You should see the event come down:

```
$ wscat -c ws://localhost:3000
connected (press CTRL+C to quit)
< {"topic":"new client joined"}
< {"topic":"new_post","data":{"__v":0,"username":"dickeyxxx","body":
→ "new status update!","_id":"53d462728ab571000037f17a",
→ "date":"2014-07-27T02:22:42.962Z"}}
```

Now that you have your Node server listening for WebSockets and passing events on new posts, you need to make Angular listen on the WebSocket.

WEBSOCKETS IN ANGULAR.JS

Angular does not have any built-in functionality for WebSockets, but using some of the $scope events functionality you looked at previously, it's not hard for you to handle it yourself. First, you need to write a bit of code to dispatch the WebSocket messages to interested components.

Create a file ng/websockets.js with the following:

```
angular.module('app')
.run(function ($rootScope) {
  var url = 'ws://localhost:3000'
  var connection = new WebSocket(url)

  connection.onopen = function () {
    console.log('WebSocket connected')
  }
})
```

This is an Angular run component. These simply get executed late in the initialization phase. You don't want to use a service for this because nothing will directly connect to this component; you'll simply publish events to $rootScope that a controller or service can listen to with $scope.$on(). $rootScope is like $scope except that it's the parent $scope that everything inherits from. It's also a singleton, so it can be used to share global information through an application. While sharing state is better done by having a hierarchy of ng-controller $scopes, passing global events leads to nicely decoupled asynchronous applications.

You create a connection directly to localhost:3000. You could analyze the URL and change the protocol from http to ws to support multiple hostnames.

You then attach a diagnostic function to "open" event from the WebSocket object. This whole block (the body of the function with the $rootScope parameter) should work as is. Try it in your browser and you should see "WebSocket connected" in the console. Once that is working, add a function for the message event after handling the open event:

```
connection.onmessage = function (e) {
  console.log(e)
  var payload = JSON.parse(e.data)
  $rootScope.$broadcast('ws:' + payload.topic, payload.data)
}
```

You're broadcasting this message to any $scope object in the system. You prefix the incoming WebSocket topic with ws: before turning it into an Angular event, so your new post event would be ws:new_post. This is to avoid any potential conflicts with an existing event name matching a WebSocket topic.

You're also logging out the message event. It'd be good to try posting a post and seeing whether the event pops up in the console before continuing.

What you need to do now is listen to this event in the posts controller and, upon receipt, unshift the post into $scope.posts. Inside ng/posts.ctrl.js, here is the code:

```
$scope.$on('ws:new_post', function (_, post) {
  $scope.$apply(function () {
    $scope.posts.unshift(post)
  })
})
```

Remember to also remove the other unshift for the user posting the update; otherwise, the post will appear twice. A nice side benefit of using WebSockets is that you no longer need that code (although it was just one line).

I'm not sure why $scope.$apply() is necessary here, but without it the UI won't update. I think that $scope.$on should be triggering a digest cycle, so it may be an Angular bug. Regardless, adding $scope.$apply() solves the issue.

WEBSOCKET ARCHITECTURE

WebSockets is still new technology, and we're still finding good ways to leverage it. There are some factors you certainly need to take into account when building an application with WebSockets.

RECONNECTION

In development, our Node server often restarts, killing the WebSocket. Even in production this is possible, so it's a good idea to have the client reconnect on disconnection. To accomplish this, simply wrap the connection logic in a function and call it under a $timeout a few seconds later. Here's an example:

```
angular.module('app')
.run(function ($rootScope, $timeout) {
  (function connect() {
    var url = 'ws://localhost:3000'
    var connection = new WebSocket(url)
    connection.onclose = function (e) {
      console.log('WebSocket closed. Reconnecting...')
      $timeout(connect, 10*1000)
    }
    connection.onmessage = function (e) {
      var payload = JSON.parse(e.data)
      $rootScope.$broadcast('ws:' + payload.topic, payload.data)
    }
  })()
})
```

Because the close event is called when a connection is unsuccessful, this will just keep retrying forever. You could get fancier with this and do some exponential backoff to first retry quickly but gradually reduce the reconnect frequency.

You will miss out on any events sent during this time period. As a fallback, I would use an HTTP endpoint to gather missing events if that is an issue.

FIGURE 9.1 What most
people do

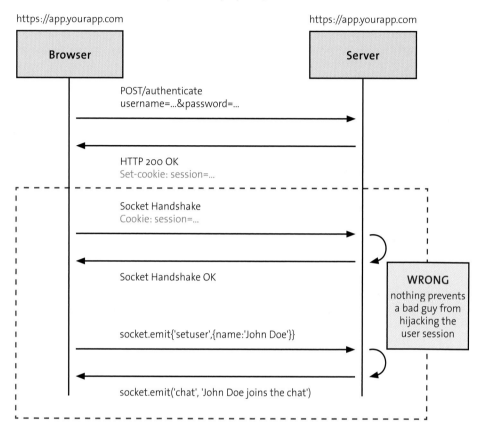

SOCKET WITH MESSAGES

(what most people do)

SECURITY

Because WebSockets can connect on the same server as the HTTP, developers often assume that the user is authenticated on either one. Commonly, the initial part of the WebSocket handshake will be secure, but then the client is free to access anything. In the HTTP world, these would all be new requests, but since WebSockets don't need a new request every time, additional security is needed.

To resolve this, use a JWT for every message the client sends up just like you do on the HTTP side (see **Figure 9.1**).

Keep this in mind when using WebSockets. It's just the sort of thing you're not used to from our stateless HTTP past.

MULTIPROCESS/MULTISERVER DESIGN

Often when developers are writing an application to use WebSockets, they will design it running on a single process on a single machine, which is not a real-world scenario. Let's imagine the social application for a bit. If you had a separate server up that was load balanced across the two, then you would have two separate arrays of users connected to each.

When a post is created, the Node server will send the event only to users connected to the same server as the one it was created on.

This is a problem you need to address even on a single-machine box. In production, you'll want to run two separate processes, causing the same problem since they have their own memory space. I've worked on a few projects that were designed like this, and it required some hefty refactoring down the road to resolve it. To catch things like this, I suggest running in multiprocess mode even in development (this is covered more in Chapter 11).

The way you enable everyone to get notifications is by publishing the event to a central location everyone is listening to. Once there, all the processes on all the servers will be notified and can reply to the correct recipients. For this, you need a message broker set up in your infrastructure. Here are the top three brokers:

- Redis's pubsub feature is certainly the most common (and easiest to set up) solution for messaging in Node.js. Redis is easy to learn and takes a short time to set up on any Unix machine. It is my go-to solution for not just messaging but also many other things (such as queuing, caching, and data storage). I find it useful for web applications of just about any size. The website has interactive documentation, so you can try every feature right in the browser. It's my top recommendation for nearly every use case.

- AMQP (RabbitMQ) certainly has the most features as a message broker. It can provide a bulletproof messaging infrastructure with tons of flexibility and scalability options. It's harder to set up and use than Redis, so I suggest it only if you know you will need it. Some of the features include fan-out messaging, replication, durability, and messaging guarantees. If you architect your platform well, these won't be necessary and can be provided by the database instead.

- ZeroMQ is somewhere in the middle of the road. It has some of the features you would find in AMQP to take advantage of complex messaging processes but is certainly simpler than AMQP. If you want to have clever messaging setups (pairing consumers together, RPC, fan-out, parallel), it might be a good option.

To replicate this error, use the boot script at `https://gist.github.com/dickeyxxx/ f9f0109d43c734fcbdf2`.

Simply put that into your codebase next to the `server.js` file and execute it. It will use Node Cluster to spawn up a new process for each CPU on your machine. If you now load multiple browsers, you should see that adding a new post will update only some of the pages.

To fix this, it would be great to have a pubsub.js module in the root of the project with a publish and subscribe function. This is how they should be used in controllers/api/posts.js:

```
pubsub.publish('new_post', post) // called after a post in created in MongoDB

// the subscribe listens to a new_post event at any time
// subscribe takes a callback that will use our existing websockets.broadcast
// function to send a message to the clients on the current process
pubsub.subscribe('new_post', function (post) {
  websockets.broadcast('new_post', post)
})
```

So long as the publish function is posting to a central message broker and subscribe is listening to it, you can implement pubsub.js any way we like. Here is an example implementation using Redis:

```
var redis = require('redis')
var client = redis.createClient()
exports.publish = function (topic, data) {
  client.publish(topic, JSON.stringify(data))
}
exports.subscribe = function (topic, cb) {
  var client = redis.createClient()
  client.subscribe(topic)
  client.on('message', function (channel, message) {
    cb(JSON.parse(message))
  })
}
```

This is a basic implementation. It creates a connection to the local Redis instance and a function publish that sends JSON to a pubsub channel.

The subscribe function will create a new connection for every subscription—Redis requires this to use pubsub. When a message is received on the channel, it is parsed as JSON and sent back to the listener. If you had multiple parts of the code listening to the same event, it would be cheaper to use EventEmitter to dispatch the events in JavaScript rather than making new TCP connections for each subscription.

To use this in a real project, you would need to be pulling the connection information from somewhere (environment variable or config.js) instead of just connecting to localhost.

Definitely remember to use some kind of pubsub with Node if you're going to be using WebSockets.

PUBLISHING EVENTS FROM THE CLIENT

I'm using HTTP for all requests in this app, but you could use WebSockets as well. An example of this might be tracking "viewed" flags on each post in the viewport of the browser for analytics. This is something that can happen totally asynchronously and shouldn't bog down the server. You can send thousands of little WebSocket frames cheaply.

To accomplish this, I would have a function on the PostsCtrl to mark a post as viewed. This would in turn tell a WebSocketSvc to deliver a message.

To build the part of the code necessary to pass events from the client, you should turn the run function into a service and give it a new function send that will look similar to the Node code:

```
angular.module('app')
.service('WebSocketSvc', function ($rootScope) {
  var connection
  this.connect = function () {
    var url = 'ws://localhost:3000'
    connection = new WebSocket(url)
    connection.onmessage = function (e) {
      var payload = JSON.parse(e.data)
      $rootScope.$broadcast('ws:' + payload.topic, payload.data)
    }
  }
  this.send = function (topic, data) {
    var json = JSON.stringify({topic: topic, data: data})
    connection.send(json)
  }
}).run(function (WebSocketSvc) {
  WebSocketSvc.connect()
})
```

Note that you should dependency inject the service into a run component. Angular lazy-loads the services when needed, but there might be a controller that wants to listen to Web-Socket events without sending them. You could add WebSocketSvc as a dependency to each, but it's a lot easier to just add this run component.

DYNAMIC WEBSOCKET HOSTNAME

The way you've configured your WebSocket service right now is hard-coded to
ws://localhost:3000. It would be good if you used the same hostname as the server
hosting the application in order to allow the application to be hosted on any host or port.

You could write a function like this to take the hostname of the page and replace the
protocol with ws or wss—depending on whether you're running over SSL.

```
function websocketHost() {
if ($window.location.protocol === "https:") {
    return "wss://" + window.location.host
  } else {
    return "ws://" + window.location.host
  }
}
```

Here is a complete example:

```
angular.module('app')
.service('WebSocketSvc', function ($rootScope) {
  function websocketHost() {
    if ($window.location.protocol === "https:") {
      return "wss://" + window.location.host
    } else {
      return "ws://" + window.location.host
    }
  }

  var connection
  this.connect = function () {
    connection = new WebSocket(websocketHost())
    connection.onmessage = function (e) {
      var payload = JSON.parse(e.data)
      $rootScope.$broadcast('ws:' + payload.topic, payload.data)
    }
  }
  this.send = function (topic, data) {
    var json = JSON.stringify({topic: topic, data: data})
    connection.send(json)
  }
}).run(function (WebSocketSvc) {
  WebSocketSvc.connect()
})
```

NEXT STEPS

Having WebSockets completes the functionality in the social application. Now that you've built a complete application, you can move on to making it production ready. In the next three chapters, you'll integrate automated testing in the application.

CHAPTER 10

Performing End-to-End Testing

In the previous chapter, you finished the core functionality of your social application by adding WebSockets for live updating. You'll now ensure the stability with your application by adding in testing. There are two types of testing you will use in your project: end-to-end tests and unit tests.

End-to-end tests, also known as integration tests or feature tests, are used to test the functionality of the application as if a user were running it. They test all the components of the application from the UI down to the database. These tests are slow but are best for catching unexpected errors. End-to-end tests will be the focus of this chapter.

Unit tests involve testing a component by itself. In Chapters 11 and 12 you will write unit tests for the Node server and Angular, respectively. Unit tests work well for test-driven development (TDD) and help ensure that an application has solid code architecture.

A well-written application makes good use of both end-to-end tests and unit tests.

SETTING UP PROTRACTOR

Protractor is a tool developed by the Angular team for running end-to-end tests in JavaScript applications. It is not limited to Angular applications, but it is specifically designed for them. It replaces the deprecated Angular Scenario Runner previously used for end-to-end tests.

Protractor is a Node.js application that uses WebDriver and Selenium to run a browser such as Firefox or Chrome. It can be used to test an application on multiple browsers, including mobile.

To get set up with Protractor, first install it in the project as a development dependency:

```
$ npm install --save-dev protractor
```

> **NOTE:** Development dependencies are for those you don't want to install on production. Protractor includes very large files for an npm package, so not having to install it on the production servers can save time during deploys.

Protractor comes with a utility for setting up WebDriver with Selenium, which is a great feature because setting that up manually is complex. Go ahead and perform that setup now:

```
$ ./node_modules/.bin/webdriver-manager update
```

You should see output like the following:

```
Updating selenium standalone
downloading http://selenium-release.storage.googleapis.com/2.42/
→ selenium-server-standalone-2.42.2.jar...
Updating chromedriver
downloading https://chromedriver.storage.googleapis.com/2.10/
→ chromedriver_mac32.zip...
chromedriver_2.10.zip downloaded to /Users/dickeyxxx/src/github.com/dickeyxxx/
→ mean-sample/node_modules/protractor/selenium/chromedriver_2.10.zip
selenium-server-standalone-2.42.2.jar downloaded to /Users/dickeyxxx/
→ src/github.com/dickeyxxx/mean-sample/node_modules/protractor/selenium/
→ selenium-server-standalone-2.42.2.jar
```

Now that you have Protractor set up, you can move on to adding a testing framework and then finally writing your first test.

JAVASCRIPT TESTING FRAMEWORKS

Protractor is just a test *runner*. It requires the use of a testing framework to actually write the tests in before it can be used. JavaScript has three main testing frameworks. Each has its own style and functionality.

- **QUnit**: This is the oldest framework in this list. It was developed for jQuery in 2008. It has been popular for a long time and trusted by many applications. Unfortunately, QUnit lacks many of the features found in newer frameworks and is rather inflexible. It also has a verbose syntax, making writing tests a chore. Asynchronous and promise-based testing is particularly challenging in QUnit—something you will do a lot of in MEAN applications.

- **Jasmine**: This was developed by Pivotal Labs as a way to bring the BDD (behavior-driven development) semantics of RSpec (a Ruby testing framework) into JavaScript. It is the choice of most Angular apps, including the Angular team. It has a much more concise syntax than QUnit, but in the 1.*x* version suffers from some of the same problems when it comes to testing asynchronous or promise-based code. Jasmine takes an opinionated approach to testing and provides most of the required tools. The 2.*x* track hasn't yet received good adoption when it comes to Angular tools, which has some of the asynchronous semantics included in Mocha.

- **Mocha**: This is the choice JavaScript testing framework of most Node applications. Mocha is flexible and allows you to pick and choose various tools to fit your project and testing style. While it's not the main language in Angular applications, it is well supported with all the Angular tools. Some of the tools in the Mocha community such as Sinon (a spy toolset) and Chai (an assertion toolset) are useful for testing MEAN applications.

It would be possible to write some of the tests in different frameworks, but it's good to stick with one for consistency. For your application, you'll go with Mocha because it has the best features for what you will need to accomplish. There are a few configuration options you need to set to enable Mocha but nothing too bad.

WRITING A BASIC PROTRACTOR TEST

The convention in JavaScript applications is to place all test code in a directory /test in the root of the project. Because you'll be testing with three different methods (end-to-end, Node server, and Angular) in the social app, you should have directories for each. Create a directory /test and then create a folder for each testing method you will use.

```
$ mkdir -p test/e2e
$ mkdir test/ng
$ mkdir test/server
```

NOTE: If you haven't seen the -p flag for mkdir before, it creates the full path if it doesn't exist rather than just the directory. In this case, it would create both the test and test/e2e directories if neither existed.

In this chapter you'll just be working with e2e (end-to-end), but I want you to see what the final structure will look like for your tests.

Now that you have the e2e directory, let's create your first test.

Feature tests such as Protractor are good for describing user stories in the system. It's good to think of using the application from a user's perspective on an entire flow. For an e-commerce website, this might mean coming to the site, finding a product, adding it to the cart, and completing the order. A test like this will hit on many parts of the application, ensuring that the common flows are always stable.

It's not necessary for feature tests to account for everything a user can do in an application. Too many feature tests can become slow, and if they are too fine grained, it can be difficult to make changes to an application. Feature tests are useful, but be judicious about them.

For the main flow in your application, you can have a test describing a user logging in and posting their first post. It's good to write it out in comments first and then replace each step with code. Create a file called test/e2e/making_a_post.spec.js.

```javascript
describe('making a post', function () {
  it('logs in and creates a new post', function () {
    // go to homepage
    // click 'login'
    // fill out and submit login form
    // submit a new post on the posts page

    // the user should now see their post as the first post on the page
  })
})
```

It's important the tests end in `.spec.js` since that's how you will tell Protractor to find the tests. It will also allow us to have `.js` files in the `test/e2e` directory that are not tests—such as utility scripts.

Mocha (much like Jasmine or RSpec) uses the BDD-style `describe` and `it` blocks. These are designed to help you document your code. `describe` blocks can be nested to give context about the test. `it` blocks are actual tests and describe what should happen during the test.

Try to think of the final assertion you want to make during the test and why I left the assertion step on its own line. In fact, a trick I've found useful is to think of the final assertion first (what should happen ultimately?) and then describe the flow backward. It can be easier to think of the flow that way since you only need to think of the prerequisites for each step.

Before you can move on, you should try to see whether you can get your test to at least run. Replace the `go to homepage` comment with the following code to tell Protractor to load the home page:

```
describe('making a post', function () {
  it('logs in and creates a new post', function () {
    browser.get('http://localhost:3000')
    // ...
```

CONFIGURING AND RUNNING PROTRACTOR

Now create a config file for Protractor to tell it you want to use Mocha for running your tests and where to find the end-to-end tests. Place this code at the root of the project in a file `protractor.conf.js`. The name and location are important.

```
exports.config = {
  framework: 'mocha',
  specs: [
    'test/e2e/**/*.spec.js'
  ],
  mochaOpts: {
    enableTimeouts: false
  }
}
```

The `enableTimeouts` setting is necessary to avoid timeout bugs with Mocha that I've found while using Protractor. It's possible they may be resolved by the time you read this book, making that setting unnecessary.

Now install Mocha into the project as a development dependency:

```
$ npm install --save-dev mocha
```

FIGURE 10.1
Protractor running
successfully with just a
`browser.get()` call

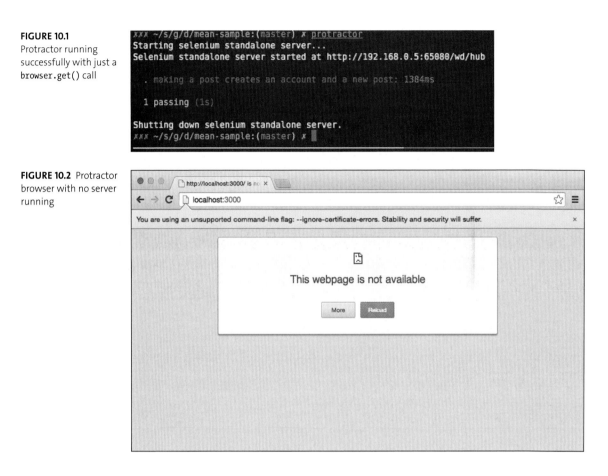

FIGURE 10.2 Protractor
browser with no server
running

Run Protractor with the following statement:

```
$ ./node_modules/.bin/protractor
```

I suggest adding `./node_modules/.bin` to your PATH environment variable. If you do that, you can just run Protractor directly.

```
$ protractor
```

If you had your server running (probably with gulp), you should've seen a new Chrome window open, then disappear quickly. It would've been accompanied with the output from Protractor shown in **Figure 10.1**.

If you hadn't started your server, you probably would've seen Chrome open with a window as shown in **Figure 10.2**.

This would've been with an error output as shown in **Figure 10.3**.

FIGURE 10.3 Protractor error when no server is running

BOOTING NODE INSIDE PROTRACTOR

It would be a pain to make sure your server is running every time you ran your Protractor tests. To prevent you from having to do that, it's helpful to have Protractor start the server itself.

Add the following onPrepare function to your protractor.conf.js config file:

```
exports.config = {
  framework: 'mocha',
  specs: [
    'test/e2e/**/*.spec.js'
  ],
  mochaOpts: {
    enableTimeouts: false
  },
  onPrepare: function () {
    require('./server')
  }
}
```

FIGURE 10.4 Protractor running its own server

```
xxx ~/s/g/d/mean-sample:(master) x vim test/e2e/making_a_post.spec.js
xxx ~/s/g/d/mean-sample:(master) x protractor
Starting selenium standalone server...
Selenium standalone server started at http://192.168.0.5:49250/wd/hub

Server 33771 listening on 3000
      making a post creates an account and a new post: mongodb connected
GET / 200 7.185 ms - 557
GET /app.css 200 3.132 ms - 25
GET /app.js 200 3.074 ms - 10243
GET /favicon.ico 200 2.565 ms - 557
GET /nav.html 200 2.480 ms - 592
Client connected
GET /posts.html 200 6.189 ms - 588
  . making a post creates an account and a new post: 777ms

  1 passing (784ms)

Shutting down selenium standalone server.
Client disconnected
xxx ~/s/g/d/mean-sample:(master) x ▊
  0        fish    fish
```

Now if you run Protractor without an existing server running, you'll see Chrome open and close accompanied by the output shown in **Figure 10.4**.

Having the server start like this comes with a new problem: The server might already be running. Because you can't have two processes listening on the same port (3000), Protractor will error out if a server is already running. To prevent you from having to pay attention to whether the server is running, it's good to start the server on an alternate port (you'll use 3001). This setup will also come in handy later for allowing you to do things differently in test mode (such as using an alternate database).

First, edit server.js to pick a port from an environment variable if it exists and 3000 otherwise (the entire file is included for completeness):

```
var express = require('express')
var bodyParser = require('body-parser')
var logger = require('morgan')
var websockets = require('./websockets')

var app = express()
app.use(bodyParser.json())
app.use(logger('dev'))

app.use(require('./auth'))
app.use('/api/posts', require('./controllers/api/posts'));
app.use('/api/sessions', require('./controllers/api/sessions'))
app.use('/api/users', require('./controllers/api/users')))
app.use(require('./controllers/static'))
```

```
var port = process.env.PORT || 3000
var server = app.listen(port, function () {
  console.log('Server', process.pid, 'listening on', port)
})
websockets.connect(server)
```

The easiest way to set that environment variable is inside the onPrepare function of protractor.conf.js:

```
exports.config = {
  framework: 'mocha',
  specs: [
    'test/e2e/**/*.spec.js'
  ],
  mochaOpts: {
    enableTimeouts: false
  },
  onPrepare: function () {
    process.env.PORT = 3001
    require('./server')
  }
}
```

Now update test/e2e/making_a_post.spec.js to point to the test server's port:

```
describe('making a post', function () {
  it('creates an account and a new post', function () {
    browser.get('http://localhost:3001')
    // ...
```

You should now be able to run both the test server and a dev server without errors.

PROTRACTOR LOCATORS

Right now your test is just loading a page. The real power of Protractor is its ability to interact with a page's DOM elements. These tools are known as *locators* in Protractor.

To use a locator, first you need to find a DOM element. Here are some of the common ways to do that:

```
// find an element using a css selector
by.css('.myclass')
// find an element with the given id
by.id('myid')
```

```
// find an element with a certain ng-model
by.model('name')
// find an element bound to the given variable
by.binding('bindingname')
```

Locators can be used to get information about DOM elements and manipulate them. Once you have located an element, you can use an action on it.

```
// click a button or link
element(by.css('.mybutton')).click()
// fill out a text input
element(by.css('.username-input')).sendKeys('dickeyxxx')
```

These actions all happen asynchronously using promises.

CLICKING THE LOGIN NAV LINK

Now you can try to add your first locator to go to the login page. First, add a CSS class to the login button in the nav bar you can use in your test. Here is what my layouts/app.html contains for the nav bar:

```
<nav class='navbar navbar-default'>
  <div class='container'>
    <ul class='nav navbar-nav'>
      <li><a class='posts' href="/">Posts</a></li>
    </ul>
    <ul ng-if='!currentUser' class='nav navbar-nav navbar-right'>
      <li><a class='register' href="/register">Register</a></li>
      <li><a class='login' href="/login">Login</a></li>
    </ul>
    <ul ng-if='currentUser' class='nav navbar-nav navbar-right'>
      <li><a class='logout' href="#" ng-click='logout()'>Logout</a></li>
    </ul>
    <p ng-if='currentUser' class="navbar-text navbar-right">
    Signed in as {{currentUser.username}}
    </p>
  </div>
</nav>
```

I've added classes to a few of the elements to make it easy to use them in Protractor tests later. The important one is the login link.

FIGURE 10.5 Social app login form

Now update your Protractor test to click the login button in test/e2e/making_a_post.spec.js:

```
describe('making a post', function () {
  it('logs in and creates new post', function () {
    browser.get('http://localhost:3001')
    element(by.css('nav .login')).click()
    // fill out and submit login form
    // submit a new post on the posts page

    // the user should now their post as the first post on the page
  })
})
```

If you run the test and it passes, that means Protractor was probably successful in finding the login button, clicking it, and going to the login form. Unfortunately, it probably happens too fast for you to be able to see it in the Chrome window Protractor creates. You could verify this by seeing /login.html loaded in the log, but a better way is to use the Protractor debugging tools.

Add a pause statement to test/e2e/making_a_post.spec.js after clicking the login button:

```
describe('making a post', function () {
  it('logs in and creates new post', function () {
    browser.get('http://localhost:3001')
    element(by.css('nav .login')).click()
    browser.pause()
    // ...
```

You should now see the login form in the browser (see **Figure 10.5**).

```
xxx ~/s/g/d/mean-sample:(master) x protractor
Starting selenium standalone server...
Selenium standalone server started at http://192.168.0.5:58844/wd/hub

Server 35749 listening on 3001
    making a post creates an account and a new post: mongodb connected
Hit SIGUSR1 - starting debugger agent.
debugger listening on port 5858
GET / 200 33.836 ms - 557
GET /app.css 200 19.010 ms - 25
GET /app.js 200 24.130 ms - 10243
GET /favicon.ico 200 47.973 ms - 557
GET /nav.html 200 24.645 ms - 652
GET /posts.html 200 22.670 ms - 588
GET /api/posts 200 148.327 ms - 19759
GET /register.html 200 6.363 ms - 446
GET /favicon.ico 304 6.718 ms - -
Starting WebDriver debugger in a child process. Pause is still beta, please report issues at github.com/
angular/protractor
------- WebDriver Debugger -------
 ready

press c to continue to the next webdriver command
press d to continue to the next debugger statement
press ^C to exit
-- WebDriver control flow schedule
 |- waiting for debugger to attach
 |---    at Context.<anonymous> (/Users/dickeyxxx/src/github.com/dickeyxxx/mean-sample/test/e2e/making_a
_post.spec.js:5:13)
wd-debug>
 0      node    vim
```

FIGURE 10.6 Protractor debugger

In addition, you'll see the Protractor debugger paused in the terminal, awaiting a command (see **Figure 10.6**).

Press d to continue the test suite. This debugging tool is great when building Protractor tests and finding problems when a test begins to fail.

ACTUALLY MAKING A POST WITH PROTRACTOR

Let's go ahead and finish test/e2e/making_a_post.spec.js with all the locators and actions needed to log in and create a post:

```
describe('making a post', function () {
  it('logs in and creates new post', function () {
    browser.get('http://localhost:3001')

    // click 'login'
    element(by.css('nav .login')).click()

    // fill out and submit login form
    element(by.model('username')).sendKeys('dickeyxxx')
```

```
element(by.model('password')).sendKeys('pass')
element(by.css('form .btn')).click()

// submit a new post on the posts page
var post = 'my new post'
element(by.model('postBody')).sendKeys(post)
element(by.css('form .btn')).click()

// the user should now their post as the first post on the page
  })
})
```

Note that I'm using generic CSS locators here as an example, but it would be good to add classes to the form buttons to click more specific elements. Not doing so might result in strange issues later with Protractor clicking form buttons you didn't intend. Running this many times might result in having too many posts in the database—resulting in slow test runs. To resolve this, you could wipe the database after each run.

WIPING THE DATABASE AFTER PROTRACTOR RUNS

Implementing this will break the test since there will no longer be a user to log in with. A better test would be to instrument the registration flow as opposed to the login flow.

To wipe the database after Protractor runs, you can use the Mongoose models inside the test. Add an afterEach filter to test/e2e/making_a_post.spec.js to accomplish this:

```
var db = require('../../db')

describe('making a post', function () {
  it('creates an account and a new post', function () {
    // ...
  })
  afterEach(function () {
    db.connection.db.dropDatabase()
  })
})
```

This works well for your application, but in another project it might not. If you need to keep some of the data around for your tests, you would be clearing it out every time. Finding out how to clear data between test runs is challenging and requires some forethought in every application. Still, this is a good starting point.

Now let's finish your feature test by adding in an expectation.

PROTRACTOR EXPECTATIONS

```
 1 passing (3s)

Shutting down selenium standalone server.
xxx ~/s/g/d/mean-sample:(master) x protractor
Starting selenium standalone server...
Selenium standalone server started at http://192.168.0.5:63140/wd/hub

Server 38956 listening on 3001
    making a post creates an account and a new post: mongodb connected
GET / 200 7.814 ms - 557
GET /app.css 200 4.207 ms - 25
GET /app.js 200 3.413 ms - 10243
GET /favicon.ico 200 1.287 ms - 557
GET /nav.html 200 1.837 ms - 652
GET /posts.html 200 4.192 ms - 594
GET /api/posts 200 11.666 ms - 2
GET /register.html 200 1.390 ms - 446
GET /favicon.ico 304 3.290 ms - -
POST /api/users 201 355.063 ms - -
POST /api/sessions 200 94.241 ms - 136
GET /api/users 200 3.868 ms - 65
GET /api/posts 304 13.460 ms - -
GET /favicon.ico 304 0.856 ms - -
POST /api/posts 201 20.709 ms - 120
@dickeyxxx my new post
    . making a post creates an account and a new post: 3153ms

 1 passing (3s)

Shutting down selenium standalone server.
xxx ~/s/g/d/mean-sample:(master) x
   0      node   fish
```

FIGURE 10.7 Logging out the latest post

Writing an expectation with Protractor requires putting together a few different tools. Your goal is to assert whether a new post is added to the page. Finding the latest post on the page is relatively easy; you could log it out to the console with the following:

```
element.all(by.css('ul.list-group li')).first().getText().then(function (text) {
    console.log(text)
})
```

Remember these Protractor actions execute asynchronously with promises; that's why you have to register a then function. You should see the console.log output in the Protractor output (see **Figure 10.7**).

Now you need to do an assertion to check whether the text is correct. While Jasmine comes with an assertion library built in, Mocha does not. There are a few different assertion libraries you can choose from, but I prefer Chai. First include it in the project as a development dependency:

```
$ npm install --save-dev chai
```

Now you can perform a Chai assertion inside test/e2e/making_a_post.spec.js:

```
var expect = require('chai').expect

describe('making a post', function () {
  it('creates an account and a new post', function () {
    browser.get('http://localhost:3001')

    // click 'login'
    element(by.css('nav .login')).click()

    // fill out and submit login form
    element(by.model('username')).sendKeys('dickeyxxx')
    element(by.model('password')).sendKeys('pass')
    element(by.css('form .btn')).click()

    // submit a new post on the posts page
    var post = 'my new post'
    element(by.model('postBody')).sendKeys(post)
    element(by.css('form .btn')).click()

    element.all(by.css('ul.list-group li')).first().getText().
    → then(function (text) {
      expect(text).to.contain(post)
    })
  })


})
```

This works, but I worry that there is a chance it might point to the wrong post since they are all posted as "my new post." You are clearing out the database each time, which should prevent that in most cases, but I'd like this to be a little more resilient against a false positive. Tack on a random number to the post you can verify against:

```
// ...
// submit a new post on the posts page
var post = 'my new post' + Math.random()
element(by.model('postBody')).sendKeys(post)
element(by.css('form .btn')).click()

element.all(by.css('ul.list-group li')).first().getText().then(function (text)
{
  expect(text).to.contain(post)
})
// ...
```

Now you are making sure that the post you're looking for is the post that you just posted.

CHAI-AS-PROMISED

Using the then syntax of the promise can get a little hairy once your tests get compli-cated. Chai has a plug-in to help make the promises a lot clearer and more semantic called chai-as-promised.

Starting with your existing assertion:

```
element.all(by.css('ul.posts li')).first().getText().then(function (text) {
  expect(text).to.contain(post)
})
```

you can replace your assertion with the following line using chai-as-promised:

```
expect(element.all(by.css('ul.list-group li')).first().getText().
→ to.eventually.contain(post)
```

Install chai-as-promised as a development dependency:

```
$ npm install --save-dev chai-as-promised
```

Then edit your expect declaration in test/e2e/making_a_post.spec.js to include chai-as-promised. The entire file is included here for completeness:

```
var chai = require('chai')
chai.use(require('chai-as-promised'))
var expect = chai.expect

describe('making a post', function () {
  it('creates an account and a new post', function () {
    browser.get('http://localhost:3001')

    // click 'login'
    element(by.css('nav .login')).click()

    // fill out and submit registration form
    element(by.model('username')).sendKeys('dickeyxxx')
    element(by.model('password')).sendKeys('pass')
    element(by.css('form .btn')).click()

    // submit a new post on the posts page
    var post = 'my new post' + Math.random()
    element(by.model('postBody')).sendKeys(post)
    element(by.css('form .btn')).click()

    expect(element.all(by.css('ul.list-group li')).first().getText().
    → to.eventually.contain(post)
  })

})
```

WHEN TO USE END-TO-END TESTS

As I mentioned earlier, end-to-end tests are best used to define the major flows a user takes in a system. These tests are slow compared to unit tests. They can be brittle and difficult to diagnose when they fail as well. For these reasons, it's best to leave it to only the major actions users take as well as actions that require the system to orchestrate many components.

These are often the best first-line-of-defense when it comes to preventing bugs from going out to users. End-to-end tests are great at preventing regressions as well since they use the system like a user, not a like a developer when it comes to unit tests. If you only get around to testing one thing in your application, I suggest it to be a couple of end-to-end tests on your major flows.

NEXT STEPS

In Chapter 11, you'll look at writing tests for the back-end Node server of your application. Chapter 12 will look at Angular tests.

CHAPTER 11

Testing the Node Server

In the previous chapter, you wrote an end-to-end test with Protractor as a way to test the full stack of the application. Now you'll look at writing more fine-grained tests for your Node server.

NOT QUITE UNIT TESTING

The tests you will be writing for the Node stack are not quite unit tests. True unit tests wouldn't perform tasks such as hitting a database back end. Writing true unit tests in Node is a laborious task and results in touchy code that requires constant updates to the test code for even simple tasks. I've found that testing Node apps at the controller level and checking for data with the models directly is a great way to build applications.

That isn't to say you can't write true unit tests with Node; you certainly could, but these tests will generally be at a somewhat higher level—although nowhere near as high-level as the Protractor tests.

Angular has powerful tools to break up the code into testable units, so in the next chapter you will be doing true unit tests.

MOCHA FOR NODE

FIGURE 11.1 Mocha default reporter

You used Mocha in the previous chapter to run your Protractor tests. You'll continue your use of Mocha, but this time you'll be using it directly. Let's get a basic test in your project just to make sure you have everything working. You'll be testing the posts controller, so let's stub out a test for that. Create a file at /test/server/controllers/api/posts.spec.js with the following:

```
var expect = require('chai').expect
var ctrl = require('../../../../controllers/api/posts')

describe('controllers.api.posts', function () {
  it('exists', function () {
    expect(ctrl).to.exist
  })
})
```

These kinds of tests aren't that useful except to make sure your test suite is working. You can verify it by running this test directly:

```
$ mocha test/server/controllers/api/posts.spec.js
```

Like your Protractor tests, though, it's useful to run a single command that will run all of your tests. To configure that in Mocha, create a file at /test/mocha.opts with the following content:

```
test/server
--recursive
```

This will default Mocha to running all the tests under /test/server. Read the Mocha documentation on more about customizing this file.

Run Mocha:

```
$ mocha
```

You should see spec output like **Figure 11.1**.

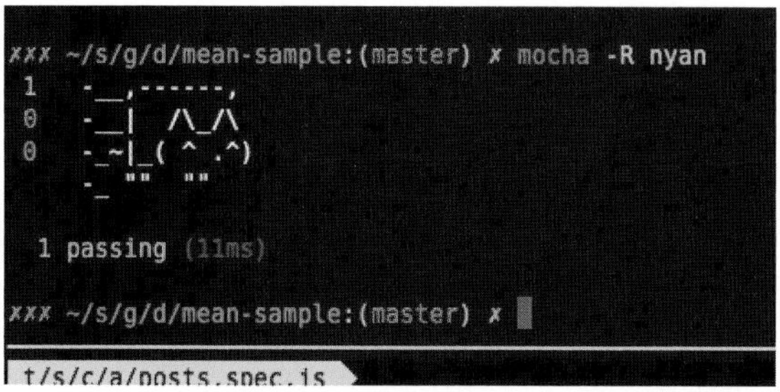

FIGURE 11.2 Mocha
Nyan Cat reporter

```
✗✗✗ ~/s/g/d/mean-sample:(master) ✗ mocha -R nyan
 1    -__,------,
 0    -__|  /\_/\
 0    -_~|_( ^ .^)
      -_  ""  ""

 1 passing (11ms)

✗✗✗ ~/s/g/d/mean-sample:(master) ✗ ▌

 t/s/c/a/posts.spec.is
```

Mocha comes included with several reporters. This one is good for seeing what parts of the code are being tested because it respects the describe and it blocks used for behavior-driven development (BDD). It can be verbose on a large test suite, though.

To see the reporters you have, run this:

```
$ mocha --reporters
```

Then to select a reporter (in this case the Nyan Cat reporter):

```
$ mocha -R nyan
```

Figure 11.2 shows the output.

The Nyan Cat reporter might look a little silly—and it is—but I've actually found it to be one of my favorite reporters for large projects since it is easy to guess when it will be finished.

POST CONTROLLER

The posts API endpoints are the core functionality of the application and the best target for you to test. As mentioned, it's good for you to test the server at the controller level. Here is a simplified version of the existing posts controller at /controllers/api/posts.js:

```
var router = require('express').Router()
var Post = require('../../models/post')

router.get('/', function (req, res, next) {
  Post.find()
  .sort('-date')
  .exec(function(err, posts) {
    if (err) { return next(err) }
    res.json(posts)
  })
})

router.post('/', function (req, res, next) {
  var post = new Post({body: req.body.body})
  post.username = req.auth.username
  post.save(function (err, post) {
    if (err) { return next(err) }
    pubsub.publish('new_post', post)
    res.status(201).json(post)
  })
})

module.exports = router
```

Imagine you want to test the GET action returning posts from the database. With Mocha, you can leverage CommonJS to pull in this file, which exports an express router. That router would be difficult to work with in a test, however. This router is intended to be consumed by an express app, not by your custom code.

SUPERTEST

The developers who created express also have a tool designed to solve this problem called SuperTest. SuperTest allows you to interact with an express router in the similar way to making HTTP calls. This gives a nice abstraction from your controller's API to your test code.

```
$ npm install --save-dev supertest
```

Here is a simple, yet full, example of using SuperTest with Mocha:

```
var request = require('supertest')
var express = require('express')
var app = express()

app.get('/user', function(req, res){
  res.status(200).send({ name: 'dickeyxxx' })
})

describe('GET /users', function () {
  it('responds with proper json', function (done) {
    request(app)
    .get('/user')
    .expect('Content-Type', /json/)
    .expect({name:'dickeyxxx'}, done)
  })
})
```

You can run this by saving it to a file and running it with the Mocha command.

The done callback is new. I mentioned in the previous chapter that Mocha has powerful asynchronous tools for writing tests, and this done callback is one of those tools. The done callback must be called within a timeout period (it defaults to 2000ms). If it isn't called, the test will fail. You use it here as the final task that SuperTest has to call after the request is returned. It's important since missing it might allow for the test to finish before assertions are run. The most common error in JavaScript testing is assertions never being run since the test completes before asynchronous tasks return those trigger assertions.

Before you can use SuperTest with your application, you'll need to do a bit of refactoring to give you a base controller.

BASE ROUTER

You can't directly add the posts controller to SuperTest because it will be missing necessary middleware such as body-parser. You also can't import the code in server.js that creates the base express app since it doesn't export the app. You need access to a base router object that is used both by SuperTest and by server.js.

Create a file controllers/index.js with the following content—taken mostly from server.js:

```
var router = require('express').Router()
var bodyParser = require('body-parser')

router.use(bodyParser.json())

router.use(require('../auth'))
router.use('/api/posts', require('./api/posts'))
router.use('/api/sessions', require('./api/sessions'))
router.use('/api/users', require('./api/users'))
router.use(require('./static'))

module.exports = router
```

Now replace server.js with the following that will use this new root router object:

```
var express = require('express')
var logger = require('morgan')
var websockets = require('./websockets')
var app = express()

app.use(logger('dev'))
app.use(require('./controllers'))

var port = process.env.PORT || 3000
var server = app.listen(port, function () {
  console.log('Server', process.pid, 'listening on', port)
})
websockets.connect(server)
```

Run your application to make sure everything still works.

Running into situations where you need to restructure code in order to make it testable is a common occurrence when building applications. This is a great example where testable code is also better code because server.js is much simpler now.

USING THE BASE ROUTER WITH SUPERTEST

Now create a test support file at test/server/support/api.js with the following:

```
var express = require('express')
var request = require('supertest')
var router = require('../../../controllers')

var app = express()
app.use(router)

module.exports = request(app)
```

This code creates a new express app using your new base router and then returns it wrapped in SuperTest.

You can now include this test file in your posts controller test to see whether the GET request is working. Replace test/server/controllers/api/post.spec.js with the following:

```
var api = require('../../support/api')

describe('controllers.api.posts', function () {
  describe('GET /api/posts', function () {
    it('exists', function (done) {
      api.get('/api/posts')
      .expect(200)
      .end(done)
    })
  })
})
```

You're actually testing the controller now. You're checking to see whether it responds with a 200 status code.

MODELS IN CONTROLLER TESTS

To improve on your current test, you should check to see whether the data the API is returning is actually the data in the database. To do this, you should clear out the posts in MongoDB and add a discrete number of posts.

Add these beforeEach filters to test/server/controllers/api/posts.spec.js:

```
var Post = require('../../../../models/post')

describe('controllers.api.posts', function () {
  beforeEach(function (done) {
    Post.remove({}, done)
  })
  describe('GET /api/posts', function () {
    beforeEach(function (done) {
      var posts = [
        {body: 'post1', username: 'dickeyxxx'},
        {body: 'post2', username: 'dickeyxxx'},
        {body: 'post3', username: 'dickeyxxx'}
      ]
      Post.create(posts, done)
    })
    // ...
```

The first filter will remove all the posts from the database; then the next one will add three. Note the use of the done callback here. The done callback checks to see whether the first argument to the callback is an error (following Node convention) and, if it exists, will halt execution and output the error. This saves you a bit of code from having to write your own callbacks that check the error code.

Now you need to do an assertion to see whether there are exactly three posts returned by the API. You could change the test to look like this:

```
it('has 3 posts', function (done) {
  api.get('/api/posts')
    .expect(200)
    .expect(function (posts) {
      if (posts.body.length !== 3) {
        return "posts count should be 3"
      }
    })
  .end(done)
})
```

This works since returning a string inside a SuperTest expectation will throw an error. Still, you have Chai to clean up your assertions.

Here's a complete example of test/server/controllers/api/posts.spec.js using Chai:

```
var expect = require('chai').expect
var api = require('../../support/api')
var Post = require('../../../../models/post')

describe('controllers.api.posts', function () {
  beforeEach(function (done) {
    Post.remove({}, done)
  })
  describe('GET /api/posts', function () {

    beforeEach(function (done) {
      var posts = [
        {body: 'post1', username: 'dickeyxxx'},
        {body: 'post2', username: 'dickeyxxx'},
        {body: 'post3', username: 'dickeyxxx'}
      ]
      Post.create(posts, done)
    })

    it(has 3 posts, function (done) {
      api.get('/api/posts')
      .expect(200)
      .expect(function (response) {
        expect(response.body).to.have.length(3)
      })
      .end(done)
    })
  })
})
```

This is a clean example of testing your GET /api/posts endpoint. Now you will see how to test a more complicated endpoint such as POST /api/posts that creates a new post on behalf of the logged-in user.

TESTING CONTROLLERS WITH AUTHENTICATION

For you to test the POST /api/posts endpoint, you need to not only create a user but also get a valid JWT for that user. You could use the API to register a new user and then log in and get a JWT, but that would become slow, and many endpoints would require authentication. Using the API would also be testing more than you need to with your Node tests.

What you need is a function that creates a new user and returns you their JWT. You're going to use jsonwebtoken here.

```
$ npm install --save-dev jsonwebtoken
```

Create the file test/server/support/user.js with the following function that creates a new user and returns it in a callback with their JWT:

```
var bcrypt = require('bcrypt')
var jwt = require('jsonwebtoken')
var config = require('../../../config')
var User = require('../../../models/user')

exports.create = function (username, password, cb) {
  var user = new User({username: username})
  bcrypt.hash(password, 10, function (err, hash) {
    if (err) return cb(err)
    user.password = hash
    user.save(function (err) {
      if (err) return cb(err)
      user.token = jwt.sign({username: user.username}, config.secret)
      cb(null, user)
    })
  })
}
```

This code is taken from the sessions controller and the users controller. With this you can make authenticated calls inside your tests.

Open test/server/controllers/api/posts.spec.js and add two things. First add the user support file at the top:

```
// ...
var api = require('../../support/api')
var user = require('../../support/user')
// ...
```

Then add the following describe block for the POST endpoint test after the GET /api/posts describe block:

```
describe('POST /api/posts', function () {
  var token

  beforeEach(function (done) {
    user.create('dickeyxxx', 'pass', function (err, user) {
      token = user.token
      done(err)
    })
  })

  beforeEach(function (done) {
    api.post('/api/posts')
    .send({body: 'this is my new post'})
    .set('X-Auth', token)
    .expect(201)
    .end(done)
  })

  it('added 1 new post', function (done) {
    Post.findOne(function (err, post) {
      expect(post.body).to.equal('this is my new post')
      done(err)
    })
  })
})
```

This test is split into three sections. First you create the user and save their token in the token variable. Then you make the actual API call you're testing to POST /api/posts. Finally you grab a post from the database and see whether the body matches the body you posted.

The beforeFilter that removes all the posts in this spec is still running, so checking one post gives you good confidence that the post you added is the one you're checking against. Still, adding in some randomness like you did in the Protractor test for the post body wouldn't be a bad idea.

CODE COVERAGE

It is difficult to tell how well you're doing when it comes to writing tests without a good metric like code coverage. While code coverage won't tell you whether you're testing correctly, it will at least notify you about bits of the codebase lacking any tests. It's good to get a rough idea of what to focus on and to tell how well you're improving your test area.

The best tool I've found for test coverage with Node apps is the npm package called blanket. It integrates with Mocha and is easy to set up. To set it up, first add the package to your development dependencies:

```
$ npm install --save-dev blanket
```

Now you need to add a support file to instantiate and configure blanket. Create the file test/server/support/coverage.js:

```
var path = require('path')
var blanket = require('blanket')

blanket({
  pattern: [
    path.resolve(__dirname, '../../../controllers')
  ]
})
```

Then require it on test runs by adding it to your test/mocha.opts file:

```
test/server
--recursive
--require test/server/support/coverage
```

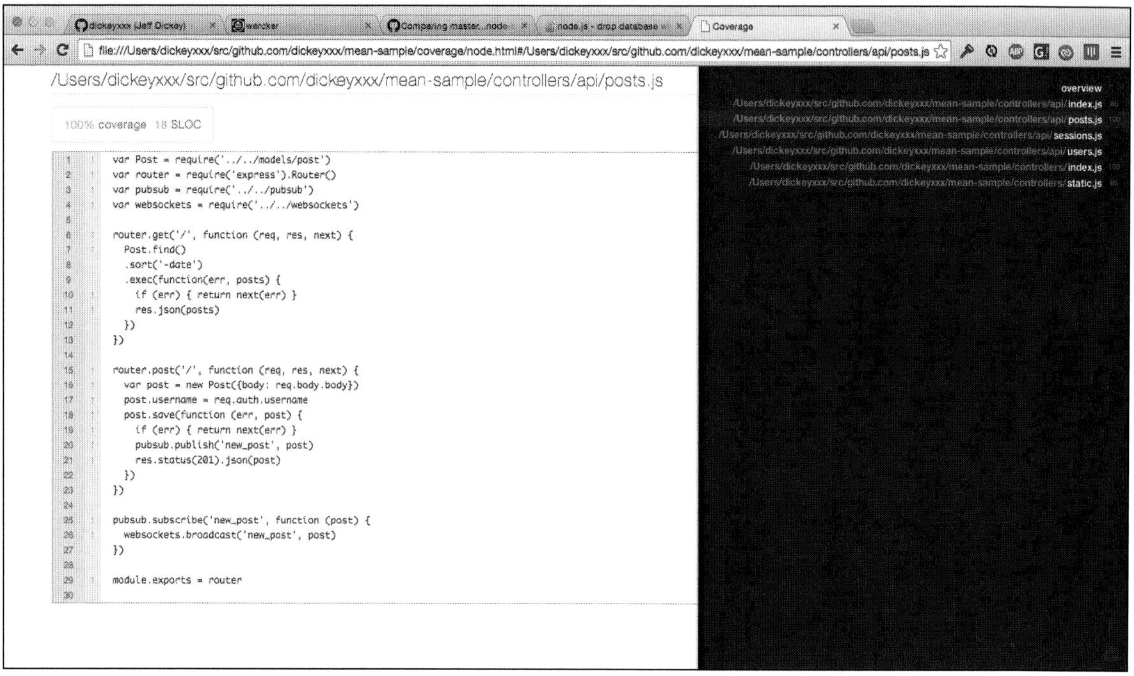

FIGURE 11.3 Code coverage with blanket

Create a report by using the new html-cov reporter in Mocha:

```
$ mocha -R html-cov > coverage.html
```

And open it with a browser (see **Figure 11.3**):

```
$ open coverage.html
```

You now see your posts controller has 100 percent code coverage!

THE NPM TEST COMMAND

Node offers a place to put the command you want to run for tests in package.json. When it is set up, you can run the test suite of any project with a package.json file by running npm test. This is a good idea since it provides documentation for how to test your project for other developers. For projects with multiple test suites (such as ours), it allows developers to easily recall the command to run all the tests. It is also useful as a continuous integration (CI) entry point.

It's a simple feature but is certainly one worth using. Add the following section to your package.json:

```
"scripts": {
  "test": "./node_modules/.bin/mocha && ./node_modules/.bin/protractor"
}
```

Then run it:

```
$ npm test
```

You should see the Node server tests run, and if they are successful, Protractor should execute afterward. && tells your shell to run the left side first, and if it returns a 0 status code, run the next.

JSHINT

Now that you have your npm test script set up, it's a good time to introduce JSHint. JSHint is a linting tool for JavaScript used for consistent syntax with JavaScript code. Unlike some languages, the JavaScript community doesn't have very solid standards on the "right" way to write code, so having a configured tool like this in each project is useful.

Install JSHint into the project as a development dependency:

```
$ npm install --save-dev jshint
```

Then add it as a step in the npm test script:

```
"scripts": {
  "test": "./node_modules/.bin/jshint . && ./node_modules/.bin/mocha
  → && ./node_modules/.bin/protractor"
}
```

Note that there is a . after JSHint.

You'll see a warning that suggests installing JSHint globally and not into the project. I suggest for this situation you do install it into the project so other developers can just run npm test and it will automatically lint any new code they've added. Generally, though, it's a good idea to run JSHint inside your text editor every time it saves—which you'll want to have JSHint installed globally for.

Running JSHint now will be slow and probably is going to result in many issues because it will look at every .js file in the directory and subdirectories (including /assets and /node_modules). You can tell JSHint to ignore files by adding a file .jshintignore in the root of the project with directories/files to ignore. Here is an example:

```
node_modules
assets
coverage
```

To further customize JSHint, you'll want to create a file .jshintrc at the root of the project. Here is a short example that configures JSHint for Node projects and no semicolons:

```
{
  "asi": true,
  "node": true
}
```

If you want different rules for different parts of the code, you can add a new .jshintrc file in a subdirectory, and that config file will take precedence. For the social app, it might make sense to have an Angular .jshintrc in /ng, a Node.js one at the root, and one for the test suites.

For more on configuring JSHint, check out the documentation at www.jshint.com. You will also find a .jshintrc file inside my sample social app project on GitHub.

NEXT STEPS

Now that you've seen how to write tests for the Node server, the next chapter will introduce you to unit testing Angular components. Unlike vanilla Node, Angular has powerful dependency injection tools that help testing components in isolation.

CHAPTER 12

Testing Angular.js

In the previous two chapters, you wrote an end-to-end test with Protractor and tests for the Node server. Now you'll look at writing tests on the client side for Angular.

USING KARMA

Much like end-to-end tests have Protractor as the runner, Angular tests make use of Karma. Karma is a test runner designed for unit testing. It can also run in multiple browsers, including Chrome, Firefox, and PhantomJS. Built by the Angular team like Protractor, Karma has a similar configuration setup and ways to run it.

The biggest difference with Karma is that you're usually not working with the DOM, so the UI isn't important. In fact, you won't even be using your layout file. For this reason, most developers run Karma under a headless client like PhantomJS. Karma is just a way to get a client-side JavaScript runtime going to start running tests.

USING BOWER

Before you will be able to do any client-side unit tests, you will need to set up Bower in your application. Bower is a tool designed to manage front-end dependencies—similar to how npm manages back-end dependencies.

It's not totally necessary to have Bower; you could just download the assets and commit them into the file. I do suggest it to keep your repo clean and lock your versions down, however.

You hadn't needed to install Bower yet because you load your third-party dependencies (currently just Angular) through the Google CDN. In Karma, you need to have these dependencies local. You'll still use the CDN for loading these assets outside of Karma, but having Bower set up is useful for dependencies not available on a public CDN.

First, install Bower globally:

```
$ npm install --global bower
```

Then create a file in the root of the project bower.json:

```
{
  "name": "social-app",
  "dependencies": {
    "angular": "~1.2.21",
    "angular-mocks": "~1.2.21",
    "angular-route": "~1.2.21"
  }
}
```

FIGURE 12.1 Bower
installing Angular
assets

Alternatively, you can run the command bower init to generate this file and see other configuration options.

Now create the other bower config file, .bowerrc, in the root of the project.

```
{
  "directory": "assets"
}
```

Without this setting, Bower would default to putting the assets into a directory bower_components. That would be okay, but having the assets in your existing assets folder allows you to reuse the static hosting code you already have. For what you'll be working with in this chapter, it doesn't matter where you install it so long you set the Karma config to point to the right location.

Once the .bowerrc and bower.json files are in place, install the bower components:

```
$ bower install
```

You should see output like in **Figure 12.1**.

Now that you have the assets on the filesystem, you can continue setting up Karma.

SETTING UP KARMA

Karma has sort of a strange method of installing. First you need to globally install the karma-cli package, and then you install Karma into the project:

```
$ npm install --global karma-cli
$ npm install --save-dev karma
```

While you're installing packages, go ahead and install some Karma plugins you'll need:

```
$ npm install --save-dev karma-chai karma-mocha karma-phantomjs-launcher
```

Now create this Karma config file at karma.conf.js:

```
module.exports = function(config) {
  config.set({
    frameworks: ['mocha', 'chai'],
    files: [
      'assets/angular/angular.js',
      'assets/angular-route/angular-route.js',
      'assets/angular-mocks/angular-mocks.js',
      'ng/**/module.js',
      'ng/**/*.js',
      'test/ng/**/*.spec.js'
    ],
    reporters: ['progress'],
    port: 9876,
    colors: true,
    logLevel: config.LOG_INFO,
    autoWatch: true,
    browsers: ['PhantomJS'],
    singleRun: false
  })
}
```

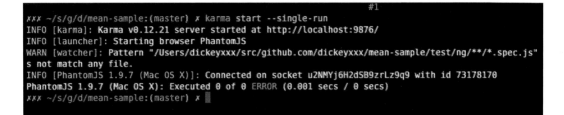

```
                                                          #1
xxx ~/s/g/d/mean-sample:(master) x karma start --single-run
INFO [karma]: Karma v0.12.21 server started at http://localhost:9876/
INFO [launcher]: Starting browser PhantomJS
WARN [watcher]: Pattern "/Users/dickeyxxx/src/github.com/dickeyxxx/mean-sample/test/ng/**/*.spec.js"
s not match any file.
INFO [PhantomJS 1.9.7 (Mac OS X)]: Connected on socket u2NMYj6H2dSB9zrLz9q9 with id 73178170
PhantomJS 1.9.7 (Mac OS X): Executed 0 of 0 ERROR (0.001 secs / 0 secs)
xxx ~/s/g/d/mean-sample:(master) x
```

FIGURE 12.2 Karma running without any tests

Most of this config is self-explanatory. You're using Mocha and Chai to write your tests. You list all of the files you want to run inside Karma (this is why you needed Bower). You then set some display options, allow autoWatch to run tests when code changes, and set the browser to the headless PhantomJS. So long as you installed all the packages from the previous step, this config should work.

Like Bower, Karma also includes a karma init command used to generate the config file. At some point, feel free to go through that configuration to explore the various options.

At this point it's a good idea to attempt to run Karma:

```
$ karma start --single-run
```

If you run Karma without the --single-run argument, Karma will continue to rerun the tests when the code changes.

You should get output saying there are no tests to run. Mine looks like **Figure 12.2**.

BASIC KARMA SERVICE TEST

Services are relatively easy to test with Karma since they typically expose a method that directly makes an HTTP call.

For reference, here is the post service you will be testing against:

```
angular.module('app')
.service('PostsSvc', function ($http) {
  this.fetch = function () {
    return $http.get('/api/posts')
  }
  this.create = function (post) {
    return $http.post('/api/posts', post)
  }
})
```

Create a file test/ng/posts.svc.spec.js with the following. This is just a simple test to see whether the fetch method exists on an instance of the PostsSvc.

```
describe('posts.svc', function () {
  beforeEach(module('app'))
  var PostsSvc

  beforeEach(inject(function (_PostsSvc_) {
    PostsSvc = _PostsSvc_
  }))

  describe('#fetch', function () {
    it('exists', function () {
      expect(PostsSvc.fetch).to.exist
    })
  })
})
```

First, you declare that you are using the app module and create a placeholder variable for an instance of the PostsSvc.

Next, you use the dependency injection to provide you with an instance of the PostsSvc and place it in your variable. The underscores around _PostsSvc_ are a trick you often see in Angular unit tests. Just like the injector when you create the service looks at the argument names to know what type of object to add in, this inject() function does the same. The underscores are optional. They're used in tests like this because you have a variable already called `PostsSvc` that you want to reuse. If you didn't use the underscores to inject the `PostsSvc`, you would have had to name your variable something different. It's just a convention used to reuse the real name of the component you're injecting.

Finally, you declare a `describe` block and an `it` block for checking whether the `fetch` method exists on the service. Note that you don't have to declare Chai like you did in Node and Protractor; adding it to `karma.conf.js` is enough to start using it in the tests.

Try running Karma again now; this test should execute successfully.

HTTP TESTING WITH KARMA

Now that you have a test, let's try to run that `fetch` method and see whether you get back any posts. Rewrite the `it` block to the following—knowing it is unlikely you would get back two from this call in any case:

```
describe('#fetch', function () {
  it('gets 2 posts', function () {
    PostsSvc.fetch().success(function (posts) {
      expect(posts).to.have.length(2)
    })
  })
})
```

You might be surprised to notice the test passes! It's passing because the assertion never gets called. You could try the done callback you used in the previous chapter for the Node, but that would just result in a timeout.

In Angular tests, you often have to call something to "flush" any awaiting events out. In this case, you have HTTP requests awaiting to be made.

Inject the `$httpBackend` into a new variable and call `flush` on it in an after filter:

```
describe('posts.svc', function () {
  beforeEach(module('app'))
  var PostsSvc, $httpBackend

  beforeEach(inject(function (_PostsSvc_, _$httpBackend_) {
    PostsSvc = _PostsSvc_
    $httpBackend = _$httpBackend_
  }))

  afterEach(function () {
    $httpBackend.flush()
  })

  describe('#fetch', function () {
    it('gets 2 posts', function () {
      PostsSvc.fetch().success(function (posts) {
        expect(posts).to.have.length(2)
      })
    })
  })
})
```

```
PhantomJS 1.9.7 (Mac OS X) posts.svc "after each" hook FAILED
        Unexpected request: GET /api/posts
        No more request expected
        Error: Unexpected request: GET /api/posts
        No more request expected
            at $httpBackend (/Users/dickeyxxx/src/github.com/dickeyxxx/mean-sample/assets/angular-mocks/angular-mocks.js:1179)
            at sendReq (/Users/dickeyxxx/src/github.com/dickeyxxx/mean-sample/assets/angular/angular.js:8316)
            at /Users/dickeyxxx/src/github.com/dickeyxxx/mean-sample/assets/angular/angular.js:8049
            at /Users/dickeyxxx/src/github.com/dickeyxxx/mean-sample/assets/angular/angular.js:11520
            at /Users/dickeyxxx/src/github.com/dickeyxxx/mean-sample/assets/angular/angular.js:11520
            at /Users/dickeyxxx/src/github.com/dickeyxxx/mean-sample/assets/angular/angular.js:11606
            at /Users/dickeyxxx/src/github.com/dickeyxxx/mean-sample/assets/angular/angular.js:12632
            at /Users/dickeyxxx/src/github.com/dickeyxxx/mean-sample/assets/angular/angular.js:12444
            at /Users/dickeyxxx/src/github.com/dickeyxxx/mean-sample/assets/angular-mocks/angular-mocks.js:1438
            at /Users/dickeyxxx/src/github.com/dickeyxxx/mean-sample/test/ng/posts.svc.spec.js:11
            at callFn (/Users/dickeyxxx/src/github.com/dickeyxxx/mean-sample/node_modules/mocha/mocha.js:4379)
            at /Users/dickeyxxx/src/github.com/dickeyxxx/mean-sample/node_modules/mocha/mocha.js:4372
            at next (/Users/dickeyxxx/src/github.com/dickeyxxx/mean-sample/node_modules/mocha/mocha.js:4672)
            at /Users/dickeyxxx/src/github.com/dickeyxxx/mean-sample/node_modules/mocha/mocha.js:4676
            at timeslice (/Users/dickeyxxx/src/github.com/dickeyxxx/mean-sample/node_modules/mocha/mocha.js:5896)
PhantomJS 1.9.7 (Mac OS X): Executed 2 of 1 (1 FAILED) (0.013 secs / 0.003 secs)
```

FIGURE 12.3 $httpBackend receiving an unexpected request

Notice you're using the underscore name of the function argument again, so you can name your variable $httpBackend and not something else.

Thankfully, this code will actually fail, although not because of your assertion (see **Figure 12.3**).

This is happening because when inside a test suite, Angular does not allow you to make any HTTP calls at all. Every call needs to be stubbed out. This is a great feature because it ensures you're stubbing out all HTTP features correctly, keeping the test suite fast and free of flaky APIs.

What you need to do is stub out the call to /api/posts and tell it what to return. Modify the #fetch describe block to include the following code:

```
describe('#fetch', function () {
  beforeEach(function () {
    $httpBackend.expect('GET', '/api/posts')
    .respond([
      {username: 'dickeyxxx', body: 'first post'},
      {username: 'dickeyxxx', body: 'second post'}
    ])
  })

  it('gets 2 posts', function () {
    PostsSvc.fetch().success(function (posts) {
      expect(posts).to.have.length(2)
    })
  })
})
```

You now have a working test for the service. It might seem like a lot of code for just one line in the service, but services tend to get tricky, and it's nice to protect the controllers from having all this HTTP logic.

As an exercise, try to implement a test for the create() method of PostsSvc as well.

KARMA CONTROLLER TEST

Testing controllers is similar to testing services. The major difference compared to the service test you just wrote is that you'll be injecting mock objects into the controller—the posts service. The other difference is that you never interact with a controller directly; you interact with the $scope just like a template would.

For reference, here is the controller you will be testing against:

```
angular.module('app')
.controller('PostsCtrl', function ($scope, PostsSvc) {
  $scope.addPost = function () {
    if ($scope.post.body) {
      PostsSvc.create({
        body: $scope.post.body
      }).success(function () {
        $scope.post.body = null
      })
    }
  }


  PostsSvc.fetch().success(function (posts) {
    $scope.posts = posts
  })


  $scope.$on('ws:new_post', function (_, post) {
    $scope.$apply(function () {
      $scope.posts.unshift(post)
    });
  })
})
```

You'll start with testing that the controller is loading the posts into the scope.

Start with this test placed at test/ng/posts.ctrl.spec.js:

```
describe('posts.ctrl', function () {
  beforeEach(module('app'))
  var $scope

  beforeEach(inject(function ($rootScope, $controller) {
    $scope = $rootScope.$new()
    $controller('PostsCtrl', {
      $scope: $scope
    })
  }))

  it('loads posts from the service', function () {
    expect($scope.posts).to.have.length(2)
  })
})
```

This test isn't functional yet, but it's the basic form a controller test will take. You again declare that we're in the app module, and, unlike the service test, you store a $scope object for reference later.

Then you inject the $rootScope and $controller utilities, calling $new on $rootScope to build a new $scope object. Then you instantiate a PostsCtrl and pass in your own dependencies for the controller to grab. Any other dependencies (like PostsSvc) just get looked up automatically.

Note that you don't use the underscores around the function argument names here. This is because you don't want to use a variable named $rootScope or $controller.

> **NOTE:** My apologies if I keep repeating the reason for the underscores, but it's something I've seen people get stuck on many times.

Finally you just check to see whether $scope.posts has two items. It doesn't; it's actually null.

To make this test functional, you need to stub out the PostsSvc for a mock version that will just return two posts every time. To do that, you just need to pass in a new object in the $controller() call. This object needs to have a method fetch that will return a promise to be fulfilled in the controller.

A pattern I've had good success with is creating an empty object and then adding the stubbed methods in a beforeEach filter. Here is an example:

```
describe('posts.ctrl', function () {
  beforeEach(module('app'))
  var $scope

  var mockPostsSvc = {}
  beforeEach(inject(function ($q) {
    mockPostsSvc.fetch = function () {
      var deferred = $q.defer()
      deferred.resolve([
        {username: 'dickeyxxx', body: 'first post'},
        {username: 'dickeyxxx', body: 'second post'}
      ])
      return deferred.promise
    }
  }))

  beforeEach(inject(function ($rootScope, $controller) {
    $scope = $rootScope.$new()
    $controller('PostsCtrl', {
      $scope: $scope,
      PostsSvc: mockPostsSvc
    })
  }))

  it('loads posts from the service', function () {
    expect($scope.posts).to.have.length(2)
  })
})
```

Again, I created a new object mockPostsSvc. In a beforeEach filter, I add the method fetch that will return a resolved promise with two posts in it. This doesn't work just yet because you're expecting an HTTP promise with a success function instead of a more vanilla then function. In order to be compatible, change the controller (the real one outside the test suite: posts.ctrl.js) to instead register the then callbacks from the service.

```
angular.module('app')
.controller('PostsCtrl', function ($scope, PostsSvc) {
  $scope.addPost = function () {
    if ($scope.pos.body) {
      PostsSvc.create({
        body: $scope.post.body
      }).then(function () {
        $scope.post.body = null
      })
    }
  }

  PostsSvc.fetch().then(function (posts) {
    $scope.posts = posts
  })

  $scope.$on('ws:new_post', function (_, post) {
    $scope.$apply(function () {
      $scope.posts.unshift(post)
    });
  })
})
```

I'll leave it as an exercise for you, but you should change the service and service tests to work with this syntax as well.

Going back to your test, it might be surprising to see that updating the controller to use the then function wasn't enough to get the test to pass; it still has a null `$scope.posts` object. That is happening because the digest events are sitting and waiting until they are flushed. You can flush them with `$scope.$digest()`. Add that line before checking to see whether there are any posts.

This should be enough for the test to pass, but just in case, here is the test file in its entirety:

```
describe('posts.ctrl', function () {
  beforeEach(module('app'))
  var $scope

  var mockPostsSvc = {}
  beforeEach(inject(function ($q) {
    mockPostsSvc.fetch = function () {
      var deferred = $q.defer()
      deferred.resolve([
        {username: 'dickeyxxx', body: 'first post'},
        {username: 'dickeyxxx', body: 'second post'}
      ])
      return deferred.promise
    }
  }))

  beforeEach(inject(function ($rootScope, $controller) {
    $scope = $rootScope.$new()
    $controller('PostsCtrl', {
      $scope: $scope,
      PostsSvc: mockPostsSvc
    })
  }))

  it('loads posts from the service', function () {
    $scope.$digest()
    expect($scope.posts).to.have.length(2)
  })
})
```

TESTING SPIES

In the tests you've built so far, you've simply been checking to see whether data has been populated. Sometimes, though, you need to check to see whether functions were called. Spies are a useful tool for this task. A *spy* wraps an existing function and can tell you whether anything has called it and with what arguments. The most popular tool for spies in JavaScript is Sinon, and Sinon integrates very well with Mocha and Chai.

First install the karma-sinon-chai plug-in:

```
$ npm install --save-dev karma-sinon-chai
```

Then add it to karma.conf.js frameworks:

```
frameworks: ['mocha', 'chai', 'sinon-chai']
```

The example test you'll be looking at is making a post in the PostsCtrl. First let's create a test case for new posts in test/ng/posts.ctrl.spec.js:

```
it('sends a new post to the service', function () {
  $scope.post = {body: 'my new post'}
  $scope.addPost()
})
```

You get a simple error in this case that there is no function create on the PostsSvc. This is happening because you're using a mock object that you never created that method for. In the before filter, where you added the fetch method, add the create method as well:

```
var mockPostsSvc = {}
beforeEach(inject(function ($q) {
  mockPostsSvc.fetch = function () {
    var deferred = $q.defer()
    deferred.resolve([
      {username: 'dickeyxxx', body: 'first post'},
      {username: 'dickeyxxx', body: 'second post'}
    ])
    return deferred.promise
  }
  mockPostsSvc.create = function () {
    var deferred = $q.defer()
    deferred.resolve()
    return deferred.promise
  }
}))
```

It doesn't matter that you're not doing anything with taking in or returning data in the stubbed create function since a spy will do that for you.

Now update the test case to wrap the create method in a spy; then check to see whether the spy was called with the correct arguments:

```
it('sends a new post to the service', function () {
  sinon.spy(mockPostsSvc, 'create')
  $scope.post = {body: 'my new post'}
  $scope.addPost()
  expect(mockPostsSvc.create).to.have.been.calledWith({body: 'my new post'})
})
```

This test should now be passing.

Sinon has much more advanced functionality when it comes to seeing how many times something was called, stubbing the results out of a function, mocking time, and more.

NEXT STEPS

Now that you've fully tested your application with end-to-end, Node, and Angular tests, you will continue hardening the application by making it production ready. Chapter 13 will examine deploying your MEAN application and taking steps to make it ready for production.

CHAPTER 13

Deploying to Heroku

The previous three chapters focused on hardening your project with automated testing. Now you'll look at deploying the application to a production environment on Heroku.

PLATFORM-AS-A-SERVICE

Heroku is a platform-as-a-service (PaaS). There are three major PaaSs available for deploying Node.js applications: Heroku, Nodejitsu, and Modulus. Enabling your application to work on a PaaS is a similar process between all these services. I'll focus on Heroku because its currently the most popular PaaS and supports many heavily trafficked Node.js applications.

A PaaS is a service that abstracts away specific servers in favor of deploying applications. Deploying an application to a PaaS is much easier than configuring individual servers to host applications.

The downside of PaaSs is that they usually have limitations on what you can do with your application. For example, most PaaSs don't allow you to interact with the local filesystem for anything other than temporary storage.

Usually these limitations are in place to prevent the developer from making bad architectural decisions. Working with a PaaS from the beginning will usually force the developer to adopt solid architecture patterns, and as such, migrating a way from a PaaS to a server-based setup is not difficult.

The other downside of a PaaS is they are more expensive per compute unit. In my experience, however, I've actually found PaaS-deployed applications to be *cheaper* than those deployed on servers because server-based setups are usually way overprovisioned—due to risk in spinning down unused resources as well as simple laziness. There isn't a lot of motivation for developers on a team to keep track of operation cost when they aren't the ones footing the bill. In contrast, PaaSs allow the operations team to fine-tune the resources, ultimately making the PaaS setup cheaper.

The main advantage of a PaaS over servers is that developers will spend less time configuring the application for production and be able to spend more time working on the application itself.

HOW HEROKU WORKS

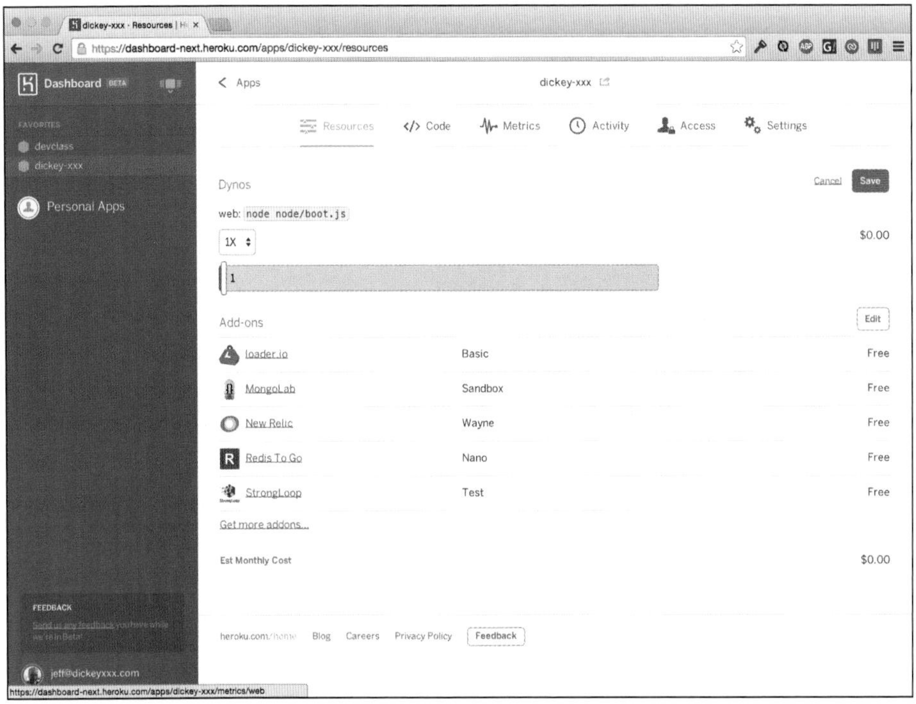

FIGURE 13.1

http://dickeyxxx.com admin interface in Heroku

Essentially Heroku provides a service to allow you to host UNIX processes (such as a Node process). Once you have one deployed, you can add more to the system simply by using a slider in the admin interface. **Figure 13.1** shows an example of the interface from my blog (a MEAN application).

As you can see, the dynos are currently set at 1 (1 being the free tier). Moving that slider would provision more processes if I needed to scale up the system.

Heroku also provides add-on services from third-party providers. For this project I'm using MongoLab as a MongoDB provider, NewRelic for performance monitoring, and Redis To Go as my Redis provider. These are all free add-ons, but if I wanted to get more performance out of one, I could upgrade the add-on and be charged via my Heroku account.

Having centralized billing for add-ons helps when running multiple environments inside an organization.

TWELVE-FACTOR APPS

Heroku coined the term *12-factor* as a methodology for building applications. Following these patterns leads to portability with an application, allowing the application to easily be deployed to multiple environments on different providers and to have development-production parity. It's a set of techniques that leads to applications that are easy to develop, deploy, test, and scale up.

Heroku applications require following the 12-factor methodology, but it's a great set of techniques useful for applications of any size.

Here are the 12 factors:

1. **Codebase**: One codebase tracked in revision control; many deploys.
2. **Dependencies**: Explicitly declare and isolate dependencies.
3. **Config**: Store config in the environment.
4. **Backing services**: Treat backing services as attached resources.
5. **Build, release, run**: Strictly separate build and run stages.
6. **Processes**: Execute the app as one or more stateless processes.
7. **Port binding**: Export services via port binding.
8. **Concurrency**: Scale out via the process model.
9. **Disposability**: Maximize robustness with fast startup and graceful shutdown.
10. **Dev/prod parity**: Keep development, staging, and production as similar as possible.
11. **Logs**: Treat logs as event streams.
12. **Admin processes**: Run admin/management tasks as one-off processes.

In my opinion, the real groundbreaking one—as well as potentially the least familiar—is factor 3: config. Having configuration exist solely in environment variables allows a developer to change back-end services behind an application simply by editing environment variables—without requiring a deploy.

It also allows private keys to not be checked into a codebase.

As you deploy our application on Heroku, you'll see how these environment variables allow you to quickly make your application production-ready. You can also learn much more about the 12-factor methodology at *http://12factor.net*.

DEPLOYING AN APPLICATION TO HEROKU

Now you'll deploy our social app to Heroku. To get started, first create a Heroku account at Heroku.com and install the tool belt (instructions will be provided after signing up).

Once that's complete, go to your application in the terminal. If you haven't turned your project into a Git repo yet, you'll need to do that now. The only way to get code on Heroku is by Git, so even if you're using a different source control tool, you'll still have to integrate Git to use Heroku.

If at any point during this process you have trouble getting the application to work and are seeing errors other than those described, clone my example repo at *https://github.com/dickeyxxx/mean-sample*. That repository will be Heroku-ready.

To turn your project into a Git repo, go to the root of the application then initialize a repo and commit all the files to it. Skip this step if you already have the project in Git.

```
$ git init
```

If you're using your own code, before you make your initial commit, you'll want to create a .gitignore file and add the following:

```
node_modules
assets
```

The Node modules will be taken care of by Heroku, as will the assets (see the "Compiling Assets" section). With that finished, commit all the files:

```
$ git commit -am "init"
```

Now that the project is in a Git repo, run the heroku create command. This will add a git remote automatically that you can use to deploy the application.

```
$ heroku create
Creating dry-sands-8759... done, stack is cedar
http://dry-sands-8759.herokuapp.com/ | git@heroku.com:dry-sands-8759.git
Git remote heroku added
```

Heroku will automatically give your project a name; in my case, that name is dry-sands-8759. These names are autogenerated, so yours will be different.

You can check to see whether the Git remote was added correctly by listing the remotes:

```
$ git remote -v
heroku  git@heroku.com:dry-sands-8759.git (fetch)
heroku  git@heroku.com:dry-sands-8759.git (push)
```

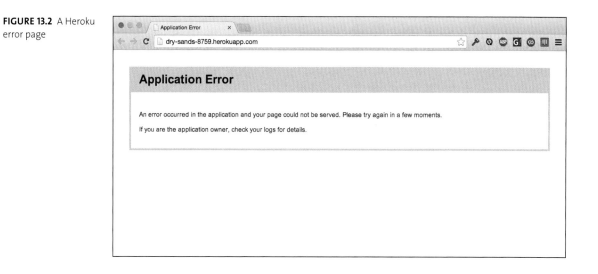

FIGURE 13.2 A Heroku error page

This is just done to ensure that the tool belt created the remote successfully. If it did, you can now attempt a deploy by pushing to it:

```
$ git push heroku master
```

You will now see Heroku attempt to compile a slug (a compressed, prepackaged copy of the application) out of the code you pushed up. It will also run npm install to install all of your dependencies, which is why we didn't commit the node_modules folder (it also keeps your repository small).

If it builds and deploys the application successfully, you'll see a message at the end saying "Deployed to Heroku." Now type heroku open to open the app in your browser.

It's likely on the first push you will get an error message like the one shown in **Figure 13.2**.

You can't tell what is wrong from this error page, so you need to look at the logs. From the terminal, type heroku logs to print out the most recent logs.

It might be hard to see, but the error I received (and likely you as well) is because Heroku is trying to connect to a nonexistent MongoDB instance on localhost.

```
Error: failed to connect to [localhost:27017]
```

MongoDB ON HEROKU

The application requires a connection to MongoDB, so let's add a MongoDB add-on and see whether you can get past this error. Typically deploying an application involves this process of seeing an error, fixing it, and then moving on to the next one.

Install MongoLab (alternatively you could also install the MongoHQ add-on and the process would be similar). Note that you will need to verify your Heroku account (add credit card information to it) before this will work. The add-on is free; requiring a credit card helps prevent abuse of the free resources.

```
$ heroku addons:add mongolab
```

Heroku provides the connection information to the application via environment variables. You can see all the environment variables either in the dashboard or with the tool belt:

```
$ heroku config
```

This will show the MONGOLAB_URI environment variable and its value. You need to modify your application to check for that MONGOLAB_URI environment variable and use it if it exists.

Modify db.js to look like the following:

```
var mongoose = require('mongoose')
var url = process.env.MONGOLAB_URI || 'mongodb://localhost/social'
mongoose.connect(url)
module.exports = mongoose
```

This is a common pattern with Heroku applications. Your app will first check an environment variable for a configuration option and, if it doesn't find it, default to a local development setting. This allows you to deploy your application in different environments without any code changes. It also allows you to change services simply by modifying environment variables and not requiring a full deploy.

REDIS ON HEROKU

This section assumes you have implemented the Redis pubsub code from Chapter 9. If you have not done so, feel free to skip or use the sample code at *https://github.com/dickeyxxx/ mean-sample* for reference.

Deploying the app again still results in an error message. If you look in the logs, however, you'll see a different error message.

```
Error: Redis connection to localhost:6379 failed - connect ECONNREFUSED
```

Redis is attempting to connect to a local Redis server and failing just like it did with MongoDB. Adding Redis is just as simple. There are a few providers, but Redis To Go is probably the easiest to set up.

```
$ heroku addons:add redistogo
```

Running heroku config again will now show you that Redis To Go put the server URL in the REDISTOGO_URL environment variable.

```
REDISTOGO_URL: redis://redistogo:xxx@hoki.redistogo.com:10062/
```

Inside pubsub.js, you have been using the default Redis client. This client unfortunately doesn't natively accept URLs for configuration like the MongoDB client does. You need to alter the code to parse the URL with Node's built-in url module.

```
var redis = require('redis')
var url = process.env.REDISTOGO_URL || 'redis://localhost:6379'
var host = require('url').parse(url)

function newClient() {
  var client = redis.createClient(host.port, host.hostname)
  if (host.auth) {
    client.auth(host.auth.split(":")[1])
  }
  return client
}
```

```
var client = newClient()

exports.publish = function (topic, data) {
  client.publish(topic, JSON.stringify(data))
}

exports.subscribe = function (topic, cb) {
  var client = newClient()
  client.subscribe(topic)
  client.on('message', function (channel, message) {
    cb(JSON.parse(message))
  })
}
```

This code will parse the URL including the authentication information. Then you define a method newClient() that will return a new Redis client with the configuration in the URL. You need to check to see whether there is authentication information (like there will be for Redistogo) and, if so, perform the auth call in Redis to authenticate the client.

You can then use that newClient() function to create a global client for publishing messages as well as a client to subscribe to each channel—in our case this is just the new_post channel you broadcast WebSocket messages from.

COMPILING ASSETS

This now deploys, but the application is missing the `assets` folder. Keeping them out of the repository will save a lot of space over time and prevents problems when lots of people are working on the same codebase. For this reason, I encourage you to keep the `assets` folder ignored in `.gitignore`. Of course, after not including them, you need to compile the assets on Heroku before the application can be started.

When you perform the Git push to Heroku, it takes time to download all the dependencies and builds a *slug* out of the ending contents. The slug is a file that Heroku uses internally to provision out new dynos for the application.

Rather than build the assets when the process starts, the better solution is to compile the assets right into the slug during the Git push heroku master step. This is easy to do with Heroku since you can leverage the `postinstall` step in npm.

In `package.json`, add the following config:

```
"scripts": {
  "start": "node boot.js",
  "postinstall": "gulp build"
}
```

After the packages are installed, gulp build will be run, and when complete, Heroku will build a slug with the full asset contents, but you won't have to commit them to the codebase. Here's an example run with gulp build in the slug compilation:

```
$ git push heroku master
Fetching repository, done.
Counting objects: 1, done.
Writing objects: 100% (1/1), 849 bytes | 0 bytes/s, done.
Total 1 (delta 0), reused 0 (delta 0)

-----> Node.js app detected
-----> Defaulting to latest stable node: 0.10.30
-----> Downloading and installing node
-----> Restoring node_modules directory from cache
-----> Pruning cached dependencies not specified in package.json
-----> Exporting config vars to environment
-----> Installing dependencies
```

```
> dry-sands-8759@0.0.0 postinstall /tmp/build_b665a110-f8c1-42e4-
→ a998-81dbcf80ebcd
> gulp build

[03:56:59] Using gulpfile /tmp/build_b665a110-f8c1-42e4-a998-
→ 81dbcf80ebcd/gulpfile.js
[03:56:59] Starting 'js'...
[03:56:59] Finished 'js' after 23 ms
[03:56:59] Starting 'css'...
[03:56:59] Finished 'css' after 3.79 ms
[03:56:59] Starting 'build'...
[03:56:59] Finished 'build' after 12 µs
-----> Caching node_modules directory for future builds
-----> Cleaning up node-gyp and npm artifacts
-----> No Procfile found; Adding npm start to new Procfile
-----> Building runtime environment
-----> Discovering process types
       Procfile declares types -> web

-----> Compressing... done, 11.3MB
-----> Launching... done, v11
       http://dry-sands-8759.herokuapp.com/ deployed to Heroku

To git@heroku.com: dry-sands-8759.git
   7407b4e..b74f874  master -> master
```

With this set up, you can keep your repository clean of compiled files.

NODE CLUSTER

This setup works, but it runs only in a single process. You can get extra performance by splitting up the server across multiple processes. Node comes with a built-in utility for load balancing a server across multiple CPUs called Node Cluster.

Using Node Cluster is easy. You just need to include the module, configure the script that needs to load, and then fork off workers. Here is a simple example that will fork off three workers. I would name this boot.js in the root of the project.

```
var cluster = require('cluster')
cluster.setupMaster({exec: __dirname + '/server.js'})
cluster.fork()
cluster.fork()
cluster.fork()
```

This will start a total of four processes: one master process and three children. Each will listen on the same TCP port and the master will automatically load balance traffic between these three servers.

A good rule of thumb for finding the most efficient way to manage a Node server is to launch a worker for each number of CPUs on the machine. It's good to play with this number a bit, though; sometimes it's good to overload a bit with an extra process or two for each CPU core, but other times it can be helpful to leave the CPUs a little extra breathing room with one less worker than there are cores.

Detecting the number and forking off one per CPU is easy:

```
var cluster = require('cluster')
var numCpus = require('os').cpus().length
cluster.setupMaster({exec: __dirname + '/server.js'})
for (var i = 0; i < numCpus; i++) {
  cluster.fork()
}
```

This boot.js script works great, but on Heroku, it is always loading server.js, which is a Node convention for a default start script. You can edit this in package.json just like you did for the postinstall step.

```
"scripts": {
  "start": "node boot.js",
  "postinstall": "gulp build"
}
```

Because this is a Node app, Heroku will pick this up and detect that it needs to run node boot.js when booting.

NEXT STEPS

Now you've built your app on a PaaS and can scale this up to support even a very large application. In the next chapter, you'll look at deploying this application onto a server where you'll have to do more configuration, but you'll be more flexible in your production setup.

CHAPTER 14

Deploying to Digital Ocean

In the previous chapter, you learned how to put the social app in production by using the PaaS Heroku. In this chapter, you'll learn how to deploy the same app to a server using Digital Ocean.

WHAT IS DIGITAL OCEAN?

Digital Ocean is a simple cloud server provider. It offers some of the lowest-cost cloud servers along with a good UI and easy-to-use tools. It is comparable to AWS or Rackspace, but I find Digital Ocean much easier to work with and cheaper as well.

Admittedly, Digital Ocean doesn't offer the same level of functionality as the others, but it's well worth the simplicity. Most of the features offered by Rackspace and AWS are easily available by other providers.

This chapter is not specific to Digital Ocean and will work similarly on any other server.

SINGLE-SERVER VS. MULTISERVER ARCHITECTURE

When deploying your software to servers, you'll need to decide what software will run on what machine. In addition, you'll need to decide which servers should be publicly accessible and which don't need to be.

For this guide you will be using a simple single-server setup that should be powerful enough for most applications, but it wouldn't be challenging to move this to a multiserver setup.

Later in this chapter I'll have some tips on what to do in order to migrate to a multiserver architecture.

FEDORA 20

I will be using Fedora 20 for this guide. All Linux distros (aside from Gentoo) are moving to `systemd` as their `init` system. Ubuntu—the most common distribution right now—has plans to move to `systemd` but hasn't yet. Ubuntu uses Upstart, which has its days numbered now that Ubuntu is moving away from it. This is the main reason for using Fedora in this chapter, but it's a great distro in any case.

`systemd` offers some significant advantages over Upstart including advanced, centralized logging; simpler configuration; faster speeds; and more features.

CREATING A SERVER

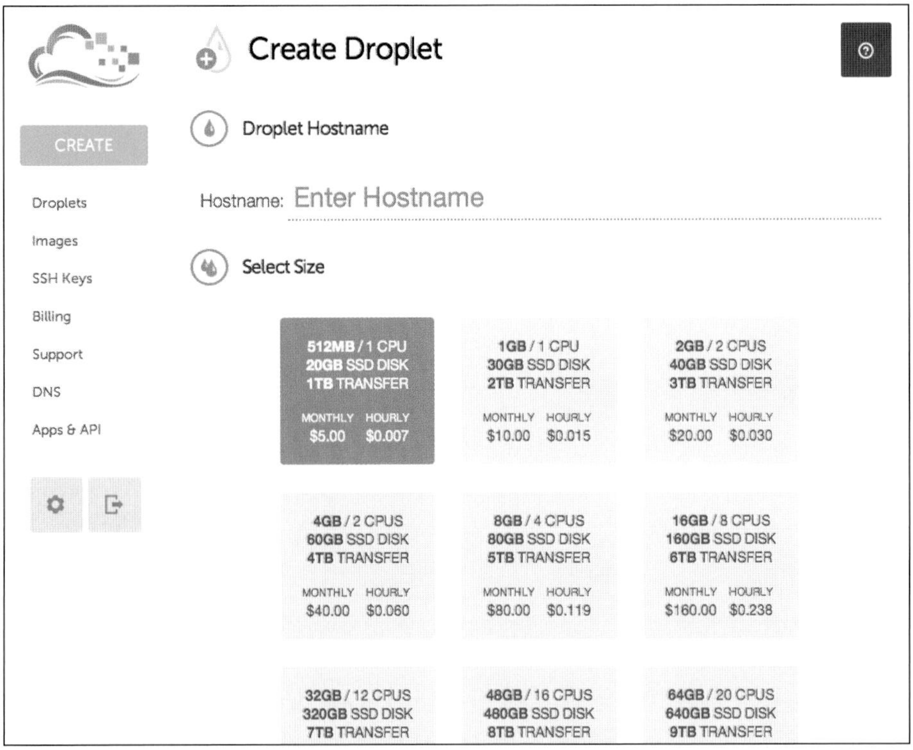

FIGURE 14.1 Creating a droplet on Digital Ocean

To get your server set up, first create an account with Digital Ocean at *http://digitalocean.com.*

Also take the time to add your SSH key to Digital Ocean. This isn't totally necessary since you can also use a root password, but it's preferable for security and ease of use.

Now create a new droplet (see **Figure 14.1**). Digital Ocean doesn't use the term *server* since it is actually a VM on a machine shared with other users. I will use the terms *droplet* and *server* interchangeably since as a developer the difference is nearly transparent.

Give it a hostname of anything you want—this is just used for reference. Then select Fedora 20 x64 as the distro (see **Figure 14.2**, on the next page).

You will now see the droplet provision; this will take about a minute (see **Figure 14.3**, on the next page).

FIGURE 14.2 Selecting
Fedora 20 x64 as the
distro

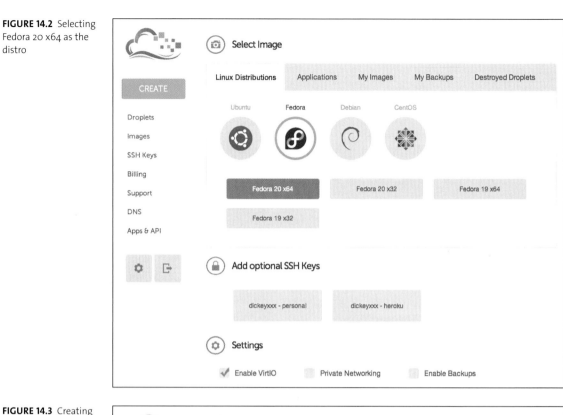

FIGURE 14.3 Creating
the droplet

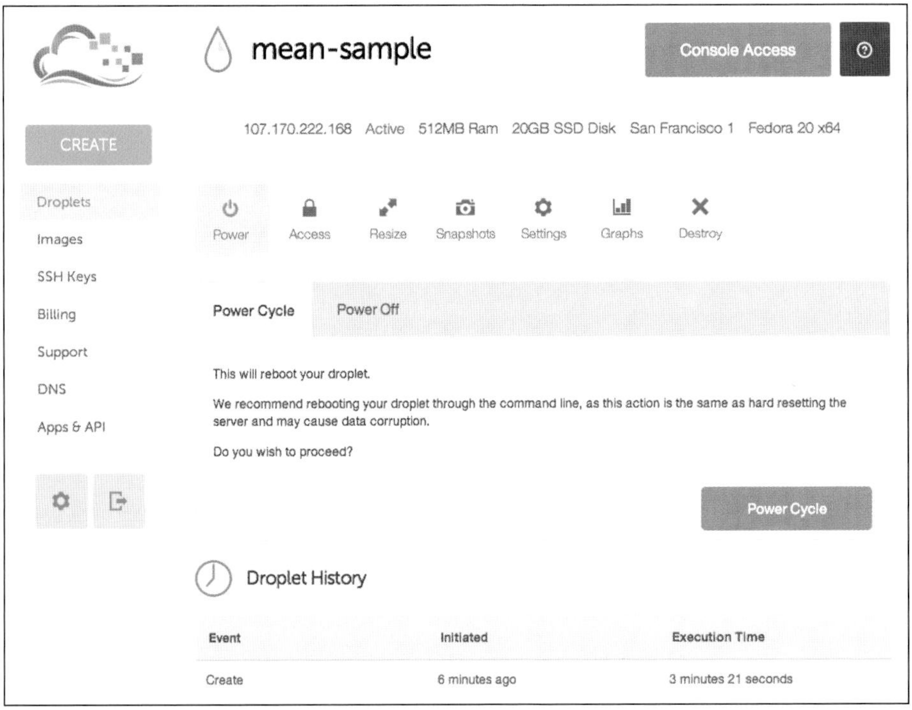

FIGURE 14.4 Droplet screen

Once it's created, you will see a screen with various information, performance graphs, configuration, and commands you can perform on the droplet (see **Figure 14.4**). The main piece of information you need is the IP address.

If you've set up your SSH key, you can now SSH into the server as root, where x.x.x.x is the real IP address.

```
$ ssh root@x.x.x.x
```

> **NOTE** You'll see a command prompt of # instead of $ whenever you should be executing commands as root.

INSTALLING NODE

Once logged into the server, you can move on to installing Node. On Fedora, you use the package manager yum to install software. Each distro will have its own package manager (such as apt-get for Ubuntu), so the particulars of the commands will change, but the overall approach is the same.

First update yum to make sure you will be installing the latest tools and that your system is up-to-date. It will take a moment.

```
# yum update
```

Then install the following (or a text editor of your choice):

```
# yum install git nodejs npm vim
```

Check to see whether these are installed successfully by checking the versions, as shown here:

```
# git --version
git version 1.9.3
# node --version
v0.10.30
```

Running --version on any Unix command is a good way to see whether it is installed correctly. Both Git and Node here are outdated versions even at the time of this writing—typical for packages in yum. Git being outdated isn't a big deal, but you should be running on the latest stable version of Node. Rather than upgrading Node, you can use the great package n to get the latest stable version. n also allows switching between versions of Node easily.

First, install n:

```
# npm install --global n
```

Now download the latest stable version of Node:

```
# n stable
```

Now that it is downloaded, you can switch to using it with the same command:

```
# n stable
# node --version
v0.10.31
```

n is also good to have in case you want to lock down to a specific Node version.

INSTALLING MongoDB

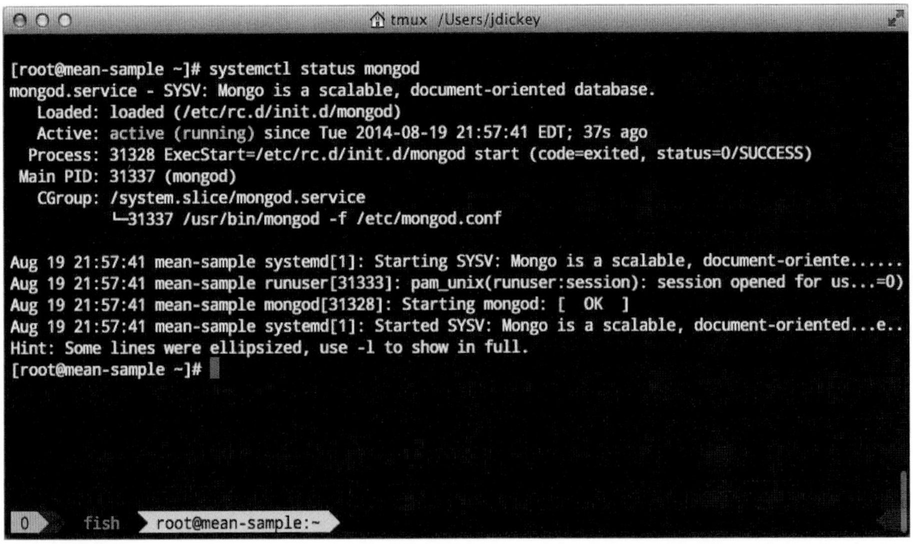

FIGURE 14.5
A MongoDB server
running under systemd

MongoDB is also in yum, but the default repository has an outdated version. To use the latest version, you need to add the official MongoDB yum repository.

Create a file called /etc/yum.repos.d/mongodb.repo with the following content:

```
[mongodb]
name=MongoDB Repository
baseurl=http://downloads-distro.mongodb.org/repo/redhat/os/x86_64/
gpgcheck=0
enabled=1
```

Then install MongoDB like so:

```
# yum install mongodb-org
```

This install comes with built-in systemd configuration used to both start the database daemon, start it on boot, and restart it if it were to crash. To turn mongod on now, tell systemd to start it.

```
# systemctl start mongod
```

You can see the status and last few log lines with the status command, as shown here:

```
# systemctl status mongod
```

Figure 14.5 shows the MongoDB server running under systemd.

You can ensure that it is running by connecting to it with the mongo command:

```
# mongo
MongoDB shell version: 2.6.4
connecting to: test
Welcome to the MongoDB shell.
For interactive help, type "help".
For more comprehensive documentation, see
        http://docs.mongodb.org/
Questions? Try the support group
        http://groups.google.com/group/mongodb-user
>
```

INSTALLING REDIS

Unlike MongoDB, the Redis team does not want to ship its software under a yum package. The preferred solution with Redis is to compile it. Fortunately, it's actually easy.

First, download the tarball to your home folder (it actually doesn't matter where you download it, though). This is the latest version as of this writing; check redis.io for the current one when you install it.

```
# wget http://download.redis.io/releases/redis-2.8.13.tar.gz
```

Then, extract it and enter the directory.

```
# tar -xzf redis-2.8.13.tar.gz
# cd redis-2.8.13
```

Now compile the C code.

```
# make
```

And run the Makefile's install step to add the binaries to /usr/local/bin.

```
# make install
```

You can now delete these files.

```
# cd ..
# rm --rf redis-2.8.13*
```

Redis is now available to you, and you could boot the server with redis-server, but that won't keep it running as a daemon like MongoDB. Because you built Redis from scratch, you need to create our own systemd configuration file.

Create the file /etc/systemd/system/redis.service with the following:

```
[Service]
ExecStart=/usr/local/bin/redis-server
Restart=always
```

This is a basic systemd configuration. It just tell systemd what command to run and that it should restart it if it were to die.

Starting Redis is now the same as with MongoDB.

```
# systemctl start redis
```

SYSTEMD COMMANDS

Here are some common commands to use with systemd:

```
systemctl daemon-reload # reloads .service files if they've changed
systemctl disable redis # shuts down redis and prevents it from
→ starting again
systemctl enable redis # re-enables a previously disabled service
systemctl start redis # starts a stopped service
systemctl restart redis # restarts a running service
systemctl status redis # shows the current info and some logs of
→ the service
journalctl -u redis # pulls down the logs of the service
```

Test your Redis install by running redis-cli, as shown here:

```
# redis-cli
127.0.0.1:6379>
```

RUNNING THE SOCIAL APP

Now that your server is provisioned with the needed services, you can move on to adding your application.

Because it is insecure to run the application as root, you will now create a user called web to actually run the application:

```
# useradd web
```

Now to ensure that you don't create any files as root, let's jump into that account to grab the code:

```
# su web
$ cd
```

cd without any arguments simply goes to the home folder—in this case /home/web.

Now grab the repository. You can use either your application or mine. This example uses my code hosted on GitHub.

```
$ git clone https://github.com/dickeyxxx/mean-sample
$ cd mean-sample
```

Now install the npm dependencies in package.json.

```
$ npm install --production
```

The --production flag isn't required but will save some time and prevent installing some of your testing code you don't need on the server.

Build the CSS and JavaScript assets with Gulp.

```
$ ./node_modules/.bin/gulp js css
```

You could install Gulp globally as root to prevent having to go into the node_modules/.bin folder to run this command. Even better would be to add this command as a postinstall step in package.json. See *https://www.npmjs.org/doc/misc/npm-scripts.html* for more information on postinstall steps and other scripts you can add to package.json.

Start the server:

```
$ node boot.js
```

You should be able to access this in your browser now by going directly to the IP address in the browser at port 3000.

If it seems to be inaccessible, you may need to run iptables --flush.

This now works, but you should run this on port 80 so you don't have to have the port in the URL.

To resolve this, you can add a simple port mapping with iptables. Run this as root.

```
$ exit
# iptables -t nat -I PREROUTING -p tcp --dport 80 -j REDIRECT --to-port 3000
```

RUNNING SOCIAL APP UNDER SYSTEMD

The problem with this setup is that as soon as the terminal session is closed or the server crashes, it won't come back up. You should run the application under systemd just like you did for Redis and MongoDB.

Create the service at /etc/systemd/system/social-app.service with the following content. The working directory might be different depending on where you installed the app.

```
[Service]
WorkingDirectory=/home/web/mean-sample
ExecStart=/usr/local/bin/node boot.js
User=web
Group=web
Restart=always
Environment='NODE_ENV=production'
StandardOutput=syslog
StandardError=syslog
SyslogIdentifier=social-app
```

Then start the service as root. The root user starts the social-app service, but the app is executed by the web user.

```
# systemctl start social-app
```

Remember to run systemctl daemon-reload if you need to make changes to the service file.

ZERO-DOWNTIME DEPLOYS

Right now the application will continue to run until it receives a restart event from systemd. If you wanted to update the code to the latest version, you would run the following commands on the server:

```
$ cd /home/web/mean-sample
$ git fetch
$ git pull origin master
# systemctl restart social-app
```

This works but will cause some downtime while the server is restarting. It will be only for a couple seconds, but if you want to deploy frequently, that could be a problem.

The way that zero-downtime deploys work is by sending a signal to the process—usually SIGHUP—that tells it to reload.

While Node doesn't come with any tools to do this automatically, it is pretty easy to listen for SIGHUP in Node.

```
process.on('SIGHUP', function() {
  console.log('SIGHUP received')
})
```

The .fork() method on a Node Cluster master will actually reread the code off-disk, allowing new workers to use new code. This means you can just listen for the SIGHUP event and then tell all the existing workers to stop while bringing new ones up.

If you call the .disconnect() method on a Node Cluster worker, it will stop receiving new TCP connections and quit when all have stopped.

Here is a full boot.js script (also at h*ttp://github.com/dickeyxxx/mean-sample*) that will both perform the Node Cluster load balancing from the previous chapter and listen for SIGHUP for a zero-downtime deploy:

```
var numCpus = require('os').cpus().length
var cluster = require('cluster')
cluster.setupMaster({exec: __dirname + '/server.js'})

// workerIds returns the node cluster index for each worker
function workerIds() { return Object.keys(cluster.workers) }
// Gets the count of active workers
function numWorkers() { return workerIds().length }
```

```
var stopping = false
// Forks off the workers unless the server is stopping
function forkNewWorkers() {
  if (!stopping) {
    for (var i = numWorkers(); i < numCpus; i++) { cluster.fork() }
  }
}

// A list of workers queued for a restart
var workersToStop = []

// Stops a single worker
// Gives 60 seconds after disconnect before SIGTERM
function stopWorker(worker) {
  console.log('stopping', worker.process.pid)
  worker.disconnect()
  var killTimer = setTimeout(function() {
    worker.kill()
  }, 60000)
  // Ensure we don't stay up just for this setTimeout
  killTimer.unref()
}

// Tell the next worker queued to restart to disconnect
// This will allow the process to finish its work
// for 60 seconds before sending SIGTERM
function stopNextWorker() {
  var i = workersToStop.pop()
  var worker = cluster.workers[i]
  if (worker) stopWorker(worker)
}

// Stops all the workers at once
function stopAllWorkers() {
  stopping = true
```

```
  console.log('stopping all workers')
  workerIds().forEach(function (id) {
    stopWorker(cluster.workers[id])
  })
}


// Worker is now listening on a port
// Once it is ready, we can signal the next worker to restart
cluster.on('listening', stopNextWorker)


// A worker has disconnected either because the process was killed
// or we are processing the workersToStop array restarting each process
// In either case, we will fork any workers needed
cluster.on('disconnect', forkNewWorkers)


// HUP signal sent to the master process should
// restart all the workers sequentially
process.on('SIGHUP', function() {
  console.log('restarting all workers')
  workersToStop = workerIds()
  stopNextWorker()
})


// Kill all the workers at once when we get the terminate signal
process.on('SIGTERM', stopAllWorkers)


// Fork off the initial workers
forkNewWorkers()
console.log('app master', process.pid, 'booted')
```

Note that this will kill connections after 60 seconds if they do not stop before then. Because you are using WebSockets, which are persistent connections, it's likely for this to happen. For this reason, it's important to ensure you have proper restarting WebSockets in place.

Try this code by putting it into the root of the project. Then restart the app.

```
# systemctl restart social-app
```

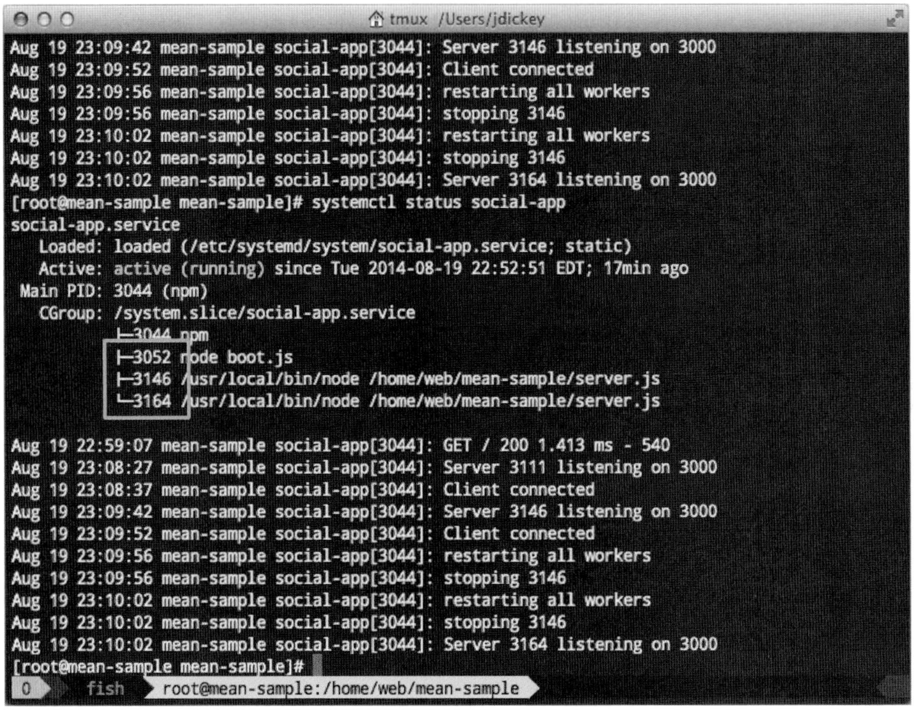

FIGURE 14.6 Social app running

```
Aug 19 23:09:42 mean-sample social-app[3044]: Server 3146 listening on 3000
Aug 19 23:09:52 mean-sample social-app[3044]: Client connected
Aug 19 23:09:56 mean-sample social-app[3044]: restarting all workers
Aug 19 23:09:56 mean-sample social-app[3044]: stopping 3146
Aug 19 23:10:02 mean-sample social-app[3044]: restarting all workers
Aug 19 23:10:02 mean-sample social-app[3044]: stopping 3146
Aug 19 23:10:02 mean-sample social-app[3044]: Server 3164 listening on 3000
[root@mean-sample mean-sample]# systemctl status social-app
social-app.service
   Loaded: loaded (/etc/systemd/system/social-app.service; static)
   Active: active (running) since Tue 2014-08-19 22:52:51 EDT; 17min ago
 Main PID: 3044 (npm)
   CGroup: /system.slice/social-app.service
           └─3044 npm
             ├─3052 node boot.js
             ├─3146 /usr/local/bin/node /home/web/mean-sample/server.js
             └─3164 /usr/local/bin/node /home/web/mean-sample/server.js

Aug 19 22:59:07 mean-sample social-app[3044]: GET / 200 1.413 ms - 540
Aug 19 23:08:27 mean-sample social-app[3044]: Server 3111 listening on 3000
Aug 19 23:08:37 mean-sample social-app[3044]: Client connected
Aug 19 23:09:42 mean-sample social-app[3044]: Server 3146 listening on 3000
Aug 19 23:09:52 mean-sample social-app[3044]: Client connected
Aug 19 23:09:56 mean-sample social-app[3044]: restarting all workers
Aug 19 23:09:56 mean-sample social-app[3044]: stopping 3146
Aug 19 23:10:02 mean-sample social-app[3044]: restarting all workers
Aug 19 23:10:02 mean-sample social-app[3044]: stopping 3146
Aug 19 23:10:02 mean-sample social-app[3044]: Server 3164 listening on 3000
[root@mean-sample mean-sample]#
  0     fish    root@mean-sample:/home/web/mean-sample
```

Now find the master PID (see **Figure 14.6**). In this case, it is 3052 with two workers: 3146 and 3164.

If you send SIGHUP directly to the process, you should see it log a restart. Note that `kill` is the Unix command to send signals, not necessarily the kill signal `SIGTERM`.

```
# kill --HUP
```

You will now see the children PIDs change, some logs from `boot.js` notifying the restarts, and any new code will now be live without any dropped requests.

Now you have to integrate this into systemd. You can use the ExecReload config to give you a reload command. Edit /etc/systemd/system/social-app.service to the following:

```
[Service]
WorkingDirectory=/home/web/mean-sample
ExecStart=/usr/local/bin/node boot.js
ExecReload=/bin/kill -HUP $MAINPID
User=web
Group=web
Restart=always
Environment='NODE_ENV=production'
StandardOutput=syslog
StandardError=syslog
SyslogIdentifier=social-app
```

Now after reloading the configuration, you can perform a hot code reload with systemctl reload:

```
# systemctl daemon-reload
# systemctl reload social-app
```

MULTISERVER MIGRATION

If you're building an app and anticipating a heavy amount of traffic, it is worth your time to set up a multiserver cluster to allow for it. Having multiple machines is also a good way to prevent downtime since you can route traffic around servers in maintenance.

A few changes would have to be made in this infrastructure to enable multiserver support. Adding another app server would not be hard; it would simply be a matter of following these same instructions on a new server. The following sections are a few of the steps that would need to be taken to achieve a multiserver system.

LOAD BALANCER

You would need to introduce a load balancer into the setup to split traffic between multiple app servers. I recommend either HAProxy or node-http-proxy for this task. HAProxy is a bullet-proof load balancer that scales well. It is a good tool with many features. It does have a configuration that takes a little while to get used to, however.

node-http-proxy is a simple HTTP proxy tool in Node that can be used to build your own load balancer. Here is an example that would balance traffic between two IP addresses with WebSocket support:

```
var httpProxy = require('http-proxy')
var http = require('http')
var proxy = httpProxy.createProxyServer()

var urls = [
  'http://107.170.225.113:3000',
  'http://107.170.225.114:3000'
]

function randomUrl() {
    return urls[Math.floor(Math.random()*urls.length)]
}

var server = http.createServer(function (req, res) {
  proxy.web(req, res, { target: randomUrl() })
})

server.on('upgrade', function (req, socket, head) {
  proxy.ws(req, socket, head, { target: randomUrl() });
})

server.listen(80)
```

As you can see, there is a bit of custom code to write here, and you would have to build functionality that comes with HAProxy—such as sticky sessions. Still, the fact that it's just JavaScript means that it's flexible in terms of how you could use it.

You could add this code into the project and then run it on a load balancer server under `systemd` like you did for the app servers.

CENTRALIZED DATABASES

Both Redis and MongoDB are currently hosted on the application box. Since you cannot have multiple databases in production (they would have their own data sets), you would need to move the servers to their own boxes.

This is even true with MongoDB's *sharding* ability (that is, the ability to spread one data set across many database servers). You need to be able to scale the database outside the application servers. You wouldn't want to require all application servers to have a local database on them—there would likely be too many database servers in this case. MongoDB is good at sharding, but doing that across too many machines is a problem.

PRIVATE NETWORKING

To set up these databases, you'll need to protect access to them. In Heroku, you were able to do this via authentication in the URL. That is one way to protect access to services, but the safer way would be via IP address. Digital Ocean offers private networking, which gives you an extra IP address to bind to that only your servers can access. It's just a matter of flipping a switch and then using that private IP addresses instead of the public one. More information on that is available here: *https://www.digitalocean.com/community/tutorials/ how-to-set-up-and-use-digitalocean-private-networking*.

You need to do either authentication or private networking if your application servers need to speak to the database servers.

NEXT STEPS

A setup like this is a great starting point for an application. You should be able to easily extend this because of how simple it is to test and iterate on different components.

I encourage you to experiment with your architecture to find out what works well for your application.

CONCLUSION

This is the end of our journey together. You've built a simple yet complete web application. This is a great place to get started building your own application on the MEAN stack. You've learned how to manage assets, build a JSON API, interact with MongoDB, integrate WebSockets, deploy to a server, and more. I encourage you to put your version of the social app on GitHub to have it for reference later.

You have the skills needed to create your own application. As you've seen, building an application on the MEAN stack is quite a bit different, but it provides you with a powerful and flexible architecture.

INDEX

NUMBER

12-factor apps. *See* Heroku 12-factor apps

A

Ajax-empowered JavaScript, 4

AMQP (RabbitMQ) message broker, 137

Angular applications

    cookie-based authentication, 88

    token-based authentication, 88

Angular code modules, 31

Angular.js. *See also* Node integration with
    Angular

    benefits, 12

    breaking into services, 64–66

    creating logical sections, 64–66

    events, 114–115

    vs. jQuery, 10–12

    JSON, 12

    overview, 10

    recent posts page, 31–33

    serving static assets, 63–64

    "Unknown provider" error, 75

    use with MEAN stack, 12

    WebSockets in, 133–134

Angular.js testing. *See also* testing
    frameworks

    Bower, 183–184

    HTTP with Karma, 189–191

    Karma, 182

    Karma controller, 192–196

    Karma service test, 187–188

    setting up Karma, 185–186

    spies, 197–198

application process, traditional, 4

asynchronous code, writing with
    promises, 52

authenticating social posts, 116–117

authentication in Express, 110–113

authentication in Node.js. *See also* Node.js

    BCrypt, 94–96

    JWT (JSON Web Token), 89–93

    with MongoDB, 97–100

    tokens, 88

automating builds. *See* Gulp

B

back end, 6

base router

    accessing for Node-server testing, 169

    using with SuperTest, 170

BCrypt hashing algorithm, 94–96

boot.js script, 229–231

Bootstrap styling, using with login
    form, 107

Bower, using with Angular, 183–184

BSON data storage, using with MongoDB,
    23–24